What others are saying about this book:

"Jeanne's keen ability to determine process methodology and sort through political administrivia makes her incredibly effective in assisting a company through change. *SPP* is a proven and effective approach to problem solving and process improvement. I have had the pleasure of working with her now with two different companies, and have seen her work succeed firsthand."

Michael Somers
Director, Customer Support
Aspect Communications

"*When Stuff Happens* is a key source of information for actually getting problems solved. Jeanne has taken her academic knowledge and combined it with her direct customer experience to achieve a methodology that really works. Written in a format that can be used, this book will benefit all who are interested in enhancing their business and in gaining competitive advantages."

Bonnie S. Kohl
Senior Manager
A large network company

"*When Stuff Happens* is a book people can use in real life. Our customers expect problems to be solved quickly and correctly—the first time. The process and tools presented here are invaluable for gaining customers' trust and participation in solving problems. If you need clear, practical help to solve complicated problems more effectively, this book should be part of your problem solving tool kit."

Jim Eller
Technical Program Manager
A large computer company

"The presentation of material is concise, to the point, and easy to understand. The book not only stresses the important things about solving problems, but explains why these things are important. One of the biggest challenges I encounter is people projecting the solution (e.g., need a new system...) as the problem. *When Stuff Happens* gives simple, well articulated instructions on how to proceed, avoiding this trap."

John P. Livingston
V.P. Manufacturing Operations and CIO
Auspex Systems

when stuff happens

When stuff happens

A Practical Guide to
Solving Problems
Permanently

Jeanne Sawyer

THE **SAWYER** PARTNERSHIP

San Jose, California

Cover design and illustrations by Chris Erkmann.
Interior design by Pete Masterson, Æonix Publishing Group,
www.aeonix.com
Index by Aubrey L. McClellan.

Publisher's Cataloging-in-Publication Data

Sawyer, Jeanne.
  When stuff happens : a practical guide to
  solving problems permanently / Jeanne Sawyer.
  San Jose, CA : The Sawyer Partnership, 2001.
    p. cm.
    LCCN: 00-191208
    ISBN 0-9700304-0-1 (pbk.)
  Includes bibliographical references and index.
    1. Problem solving. 2. Group problem
  solving. 3. Total quality management. I. Title
  HD30.29 .S29 2001
  658.4´03-dc21   00-191208

00 01 02 10 9 8 7 6 5 4 3 2 1

Printed in the United States of America.

THE SAWYER **PARTNERSHIP**
1241 Renraw Drive
San Jose, CA 95127-4418
Tel. 408-929-3622
Fax. 408-929-5515
www.SawyerPartnership.com

Contents

Preface

Does it feel like you've been spending more time solving problems than expanding your business? Does the same problem, or a similar one, trouble you again and again? Do scenarios like these sound familiar? If so, then this book is for you.

- A system upgrade isn't completed on time. Help desk technicians can't look up customer records.
- Shipments to customers are late. Everybody wastes time trying to figure out when the shipment will really occur.
- Engineers arrive at a customer site to install new equipment, but can't complete the work. The site isn't ready, and the shipment is missing essential parts.
- Your customer says your new product doesn't work; you think they don't know how to operate it properly.
- Sales reps can't seem to give customers quotes that include everything needed and have the correct price. Purchase Orders require a research effort to figure out what the customer is trying to order.

Problems like these waste the most precious resources you and your customers have: time, people, and money. Failed attempts to solve the problem result in an even bigger mess as costs rise along with tempers. Common pitfalls include making unconfirmed assumptions about what the problem really is, never addressing the correct root causes, choosing ineffective or partial solutions, and never fully executing the corrective actions. Any of these results in recurring problems.

Solving Problems Permanently^SM *(SPP)* is a special method to help individuals and teams resolve these difficult situations that anger and frustrate everyone involved. In *When Stuff Happens*, I explain the techniques I've developed in years of helping consulting clients and students solve these ugly problems. Rather than a general tool box, *SPP* is an integrated approach to problem solving. I show how to use specific tools in the context of the problem solving process so you can focus your energy on the problem, its causes and, most importantly, its solution.

This practical guide leads the reader through solving a problem from start to finish. You will learn to
- Define a problem clearly,
- Organize your problem solving project,
- Analyze the problem to identify the root causes,
- Solve the problem by taking corrective action, and
- Prove the problem is really solved by measuring the results.

SPP uses specially selected standard tools and provides a means and structure to apply them. The combination of step-by-step instructions, templates, and checklists makes it easy for the problem solver to

- Resolve problems more quickly when they occur,
- Prevent future problems,
- Reduce finger-pointing and blaming,
- Assign responsibility for specific corrective action, and
- Understand clearly "who does what to whom" to make things happen in their work environment.

Your end result from using *SPP* is improved productivity for everyone who is affected by the problem. The impact touches not only you but also your customers and their end users.

Let me know how these methods work for you, what improvements you discover and what results you achieve!

Jeanne Sawyer

jsawyer@SawyerPartnership.com

San Jose, CA

Acknowledgments

I'm no different from any other writer: I didn't do it alone. This book would not exist without the help and support of many friends and colleagues who did everything from helping me write clearly to proving *SPP* works by using it to make a difference in their companies.

These special people include Sam Boyd, Malcolm Northrup, Fred Moreno, Miriam Clifford, Henry Sawyer, Lori Trippel, Peter Meyer and, most of all, the students in my workshops. These students first suggested I write this book, and I can depend on them to keep asking questions and challenging me to further develop these ideas.

Thanks also to those who contributed the case studies—you know who you are. The people who turned the manuscript into a book and The Sawyer Partnership into a publisher also deserve thanks, especially Raleigh Pinskey, Stephen Power, Chris Erkmann and Pete Masterson.

Any mistakes are, of course, mine and remain in spite of these people's best efforts. Thank you all for helping make it happen, and making it fun.

Getting Started

What is *Solving Problems Permanently*[SM]?

*S*olving *Problems Permanently*[SM] or *SPP* is a basic set of procedures and tools you can use to solve complicated problems quickly and effectively, especially those that occur in today's high-tech business environment. *SPP* centers around standard root cause analysis (RCA) techniques, expanded to cover the entire problem solving process.

Complicated problems are really systems of interrelated problems, or *messes*. You solve a mess by using *SPP* methods to untangle it. Regular trouble-shooting techniques don't work very well. These systems of interconnected problems typically include multiple technical problems as well as business and political issues, involve multiple companies, and increasingly are worldwide in scope.

You can use *SPP* to solve problems by yourself, but the techniques are especially designed to help a team be effective. Messes have many tangled strands: multiple technical problems, business and political issues, the concerns of more than one company, considerations resulting from international scope, etc. A team can often unravel these best because the members can bring a wide variety of experience and perspective to the table.

How to Use This Book

If you're reading this book, you may already be ensnared in a mess that needs an immediate solution. It's been designed for you to work on your problem as you read: start applying the steps to your problem as you go.

Each step begins with an explanation of the procedures and tools you'll use for that step in solving your problem. The general explanation includes hints and things to watch out for. Flow charts are used to diagram the procedures and to help keep track of which step you're on. The *Solving Problems Permanently^{SM}* Process Flow shows the overall process. Additional charts show the details within the steps of the overall process. All of the charts are coded: a box with a heavy border indicates the step you are about to do, while a box shaded gray indicates a completed step.

Two case studies are included to help you understand how to apply *SPP* to a problem and to show what the results of each step should be. Read the examples to follow the *SPP* process. Then comes a section called "Do It For Real." This section is a specific guide to lead you through the work on your own, real problem.

Of course you can read ahead if you want a preview of where we're going, but don't let reading delay you from tackling an important problem right now. Go on to the next step when you've finished the current step—or think you have.

You'll probably find that you have to back up sometimes and repeat a step. That's a normal part of the problem solving process: as you learn more about the problem and its causes, you'll find you need to rethink earlier ideas.

The Appendix has some tools you can use to make problem solving easier. These include a worksheet template and a checklist to help you verify that you've really completed everything. There is also a glossary of special terms and a reading list.

The Case Studies

Two case studies will be followed through the book to demonstrate how to apply *SPP* to a problem and to show what your documentation might look like as you proceed through the *SPP* process. Both are based on real problems that occurred in companies similar to the ones described. The first is a situation in a small manufacturing company; the second, in a large, multi-state telephone company.

Case 1: On-time Shipping Problem.

Clean Room Furnishings (CRF) is a small manufacturing company with about 70 employees. CRF makes stainless steel tables, carts and other equipment for clean rooms where near-perfect elimination of environmental contaminants is required. Although most orders are for standard products, many require custom products that are designed and built to meet particular customer specifications.

Late shipments can be very expensive for CRF's customers, who have been increasingly vocal about how frequently this has been occurring. These customer complaints prompt the President to tell you, the Operations Director, to "fix the problem." It's November 1 when this happens.

Case 2: On-time Software Installation Problem.

BigTel, which provides telephone services for a multistate region, has just installed a major new application for directory assistance. It has a number of features that will make it easier and faster for the operators to find listings—but only if it's working.

Directory assistance is provided to customers twenty-four hours a day, seven days a week. However, it is much less busy at night, so changes are generally installed then. All systems are supposed to be back in full production by 6:00 A.M. when call volume starts to increase, and preferably earlier.

If the application is not available or does not function correctly, operators cannot find listings for customers, who are likely to complain to senior executives at BigTel as well as to the Public Utilities Commission. Of course, the unhappiness will also be reflected in the customer satisfaction survey. The Commission considers survey results in deciding whether to approve rate increases, and BigTel is about to ask for one. Also, BigTel awards executive bonuses based on customer satisfaction.

BigTel has purchased the system from a software company called DA Systems (DAS), which is also providing the hardware and acting as the system integrator for this installation. BigTel has never used this type of computer system network before. The network includes five mainframe systems located in four states with thousands of operator workstations.

BigTel has identified a recurring problem that is undermining the ability of their operators to provide excellent service. Whenever new software releases are installed, something always seems to go wrong, and the system is rarely back in production by the announced time. When the system is down, calls cannot be satisfied, which is frustrating to customers and operators alike. BigTel has been declaring that they cannot afford this problem, and the site managers have discussed it with DAS at the weekly status meeting, but nothing has changed.

The worst event ever occurred last week. DAS installed a major new software release that included some key new features along with some important bug fixes. At the same time they

> *HINT: Whatever you do, do it on purpose.*
> Doing nothing is a wimpy way to decide not to solve the problem. It's healthier for your career to
> - Decide consciously if you'll tackle a particular problem,
> - Know why you made your decision, and
> - Be able to explain it.

increased the disk storage on one of the systems. Everything seemed to be going smoothly at first, but then the problems started. The system was not back in production until noon—six hours late!

The Senior Vice President of the Operator Services Division has assigned you to make sure such a fiasco doesn't happen again.

The *SPP* Process

You'll use the *SPP* process every time you have a problem that's neither simple nor obvious. If it's a burned out lightbulb, change it—but also be sure that's really all it is or you'll be changing bulbs again very soon.

As you follow the steps, you may also discover that the problem is not important enough to be worth investing such an intense effort, or you may identify other reasons to stop working on it. *SPP* is designed to help you determine early in the problem solving effort if you're wasting your time and should move on to something else. By deciding explicitly, you make sure you solve the problems that are most urgent and aren't distracted by the ones that are less important.

Solving a problem always requires that you complete all the steps in *SPP*. It's often necessary to revisit steps as you understand the problem better. The following flow chart represents the basic steps you'll follow.

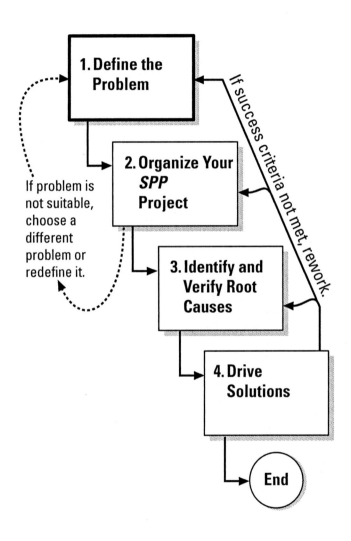

Solving Problems Permanently[SM] Process Flow

Define the Problem

The first and most important step in the *SPP* process is creating a *problem statement*, the written definition of your problem. This helps you be sure you understand exactly what the problem is— and that the whole team is understanding it the same way. In addition, the problem statement determines everything else you'll do (or not do).

Writing the problem down forces you to describe it carefully, completely and unambiguously. The statement is a valuable tool to help focus your team on the real problem and avoid wasting time on extraneous issues.

The written statement is also used as a "sales tool" to explain what problem you're solving and why it's important. You use it to make sure you have the support you'll need from your manager, customer and any other key players. This is especially important if the significance of the problem is not universally understood.

The *problem worksheet* is a tool for creating well-structured problem statements and includes the following sections:

- Problem Description
- Sponsor
- Analyst
- Success Criteria
- Key Characteristics
- Risks, Vulnerabilities and Dependencies.

It's easiest to write the problem statement starting with the Problem Description. Then work back and forth among the sections until you're satisfied that the statement really describes the problem. Don't panic: the whole thing should be only one or two pages long, and you're not writing poetry. The goal is clarity rather than creativity.

> HINT: The problem statement should be self-explanatory. Someone should be able to read the problem statement and, with no other information, understand what problem you're going to solve.

You may need to collect additional information about the problem to be able to complete the worksheet. A typical approach is to make a preliminary draft to sort out your ideas and figure out what you don't know. Then do whatever investigation is necessary to be sure you understand the problem thoroughly. Finally, revise the worksheet until it states clearly what the problem is.

The investigation could include interviewing participants, collecting measurements, creating flowcharts of what happened, etc. The purpose is to make sure your worksheet accurately identifies and describes the real problem.

You are ready to go on to the next chapter when everybody who reads your problem statement, including you, understands what will be different when the problem is solved, and your team agrees that it describes the correct problem. In some cases you may even want a formal sign-off from the problem sponsor and your manager before you proceed.

The remainder of this chapter will walk you through completing each section of the worksheet using the template shown below. We'll follow the two case studies as examples of how to build the worksheet. Then the "Do It For Real" section will guide you through creating a worksheet for your own problem.

Solving Problems Permanently[SM]
Problem Worksheet

Problem Description

Sponsor

Analyst

Success Criteria

Key Characteristics

Who (key players)

Where

When

Risks and Vulnerabilities

Risks

Vulnerabilities

Dependencies

The steps for defining your problem are as follows.

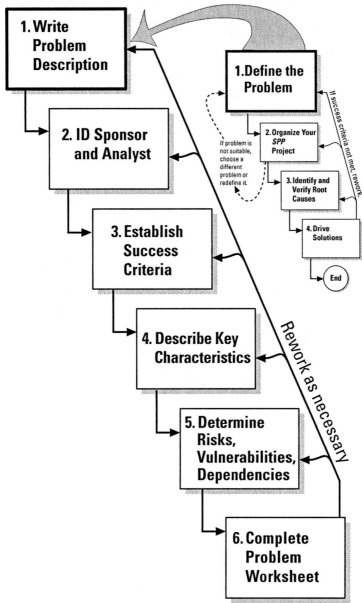

Defining Problems Process Flow

Write the Problem Description

This section of the problem statement is where you explain exactly what the focus of your problem solving effort is. This is the "what" part of *SPP*, so resist the temptation to talk about the "how." You'll always start with

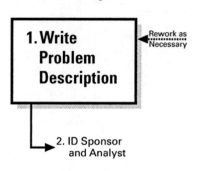

Defining Problems Process Segment

a topic sentence that conveys the essence of the problem, then add a few more sentences or bullets to explain it further. Use whatever format you consider easiest to understand.

HINT: Use SPP proactively to prevent problems.
You can use these same techniques to analyze "close calls" or potential problems, then take preventive action.

HINT: The problem description should make it clear why the problem is a problem.

Get the topic sentence by describing what went wrong. Be sure to describe the problem in terms of what happened, *not* how you think you might solve it. This is tricky, but critically important! Being careful here gets you started on the right path—everything else you do will be based on your problem description.

Describe the impact the problem has on your business and your customer's business. Describe what symptoms were observed. These are the things that someone *knows* at this point in the problem solving process. If the someone is not you, you need to do some research to find out. No guesses or assumptions allowed: the problem description must give the facts clearly and accurately.

You want everyone who reads it to understand what the problem is and why it's important. No jumping ahead, either: you don't know yet what caused the problem much less what you will do to fix it.

Once you get the topic sentence, add more statements to define the boundaries of the problem and the inter-connections to other problems. Be clear and specific about what you will (and won't) address in *this* problem solving project. You don't want your boss to think you're going to solve world hunger when you're working on just the local community.

Exercise

Are the following good topic sentences for a problem description? Why or why not? Think about it yourself before you read my answers.

1. Customer ABC is unhappy with service quality.
2. New releases are not installed within the scheduled time.
3. The number of calls handled by the help desk is increasing disproportionately to growth.
4. Need to eliminate anything that causes unscheduled workstation outages.
5. No place on screen for order clerk to enter a customer-requested delivery date.

> HINT: Words like "anything,"
> "everything," and "all" are red
> flags in a problem description.
> They start to set an expectation
> for results that are usually far
> broader than you intend and
> quite likely would be impossible
> to deliver.

The first and fourth are so general they give you no real sense of what the problem is. The second and third are good because they give you a basic understanding of the problem when you read them. They are clear and specific. The rest of the description will fill in the details.

The fifth is really a solution to something, though it's not clear what. There must be some reason why the place on the screen is needed. The problem description should explain the problem, i.e., what happens because the delivery date is not there. You may find later that adding it to the screen is indeed the best solution, but you can't know that until you define and analyze the problem.

Now let's see how this step was handled in our case studies.

Case 1: On-time Shipping Problem

Although the President of CRF has just given you the assignment, you've known for a while that late shipments have increased to where customers are seriously dissatisfied. You made some attempts to solve the problem, but have only managed small improvements. The President's involvement has now emphasized the importance of the problem and the need to find a solution quickly. It's time to use *SPP*.

You start by setting up a meeting with your production team specifically to start working on this problem. The production team is an already established team that handles all kinds of production problems, so this assignment fits right in with their charter. In the meeting, you write down on a whiteboard:

Shipments are late because of parts shortages and sales setting unreasonable delivery dates. Customer satisfaction is decreasing.

The group starts talking about it. Someone reminds you that you don't know yet whether parts shortages are really a cause of the problem. This is true, so you eliminate the assumptions about causes since they don't belong in problem descriptions. The statement now says:

Shipments are late. Customer satisfaction is decreasing.

Everyone agrees that this is on the right track, but it's still not quite right since you don't actually know if shipments are late or if customers have a different expectation than CRF of when the shipment is due. However, you do know that customers are complaining about late shipments, so you decide to start with that:

Customers are complaining that shipments are frequently late.

Further discussion makes you realize that the problem isn't just late shipments because customers include incomplete and incorrect shipments as part of being late. Your topic sentence becomes:

Customers are complaining that shipments
are frequently late, incomplete or incorrect.

Further discussion about the problem brings out concerns about accommodating last-minute changes. The team agrees that any solution must allow customer-initiated changes, but that changes initiated by CRF (e.g., to change suppliers, modify design, etc.) should not be allowed to cause a late shipment.

You agree on the descripton and write it on your worksheet:

Solving Problems Permanently^{SM}
Problem Worksheet

Problem Description

Customers are complaining that shipments are frequently late, incomplete or simply incorrect. They are unhappy as these delays are expensive and impact their ability to serve their customers.

On-time, correct shipments are necessary, but CRF must remain flexible to accommodate last-minute customer changes and special requirements. Handling returns and redoing incorrect orders is also expensive for CRF.

- *(form continues)* -

The problem description makes it clear that the problem is not only getting orders shipped on time, but also getting them complete and correct. The description also emphasizes that this is an expensive problem for both customers and CRF. You don't have to know more than this to understand why the President wants it fixed!

Case 2: On-time Software Installation Problem

Although it's tempting to blame the software provider and system integrator, DAS, for the problem and demand that they solve it, you're smart enough to realize that accusations won't get the results you need. Plus there's a good chance the problem isn't solely DAS's. You set up a joint problem solving team with people from both BigTel and DAS.

At the first meeting, you explain the seriousness of the problem and why it's important for both companies to work together to solve it. Then you start working on the problem description by writing on the whiteboard:

Installation of new releases is rarely completed in the scheduled time.

Then you ask for other ideas. The group quickly adds the following possibilities, using brainstorming:

New installations aren't planned or scheduled properly.

DAS techs don't work quickly enough.

BigTel allows insufficient time for installations.

DAS releases buggy software.

After further carefully moderated discussion, the group agrees that the first statement best expresses the heart of the problem. The rest of the proposed topic sentences, although possibly true, make assumptions about why the installations weren't completed on time.

With a topic sentence selected, the team decides the

description should be very specific about what is included in an installation and what is meant by "completed." They also decide to include a statement about the consequences of the problem. The final description becomes:

Solving Problems Permanently^{SM}
Problem Worksheet

Problem Description

Installation of new releases is rarely completed in the scheduled time. Both operators and customers get angry and frustrated when the system is not available as planned. BigTel loses money and credibility.

Installation includes all software (application, operating system) on all equipment including mainframes, networking equipment and workstations. "Completed" means fully back in production such that operators can perform their normal duties.

- - - - - - - - - - - - - - - - - - - *(form continues)* - - - - - - - - - - - - - - - - - - -

The problem description explains what the basic problem is—getting software releases done on time—but lets the reader know right away that this is an expensive and visible problem. The description also makes it clear that performance must be perfect. This is a case where "all" really means "all."

Do It For Real

Before proceeding further, write the description for your own problem. Make a template for yourself on your computer or photocopy the model in the Appendix.

If you already have a team, do the following steps as a group. If you don't have a team yet, which is likely if you've just become aware of a problem, follow the steps yourself or find a colleague or two to help you think it through. It will help you get the team focused more quickly later.

1. Brainstorm possible topic sentences. Write down all the possibilities you can think of without discussing the merits of them. The point is to capture the range of possible ways to think about your problem.

2. Discuss the pros and cons of each possible topic sentence. Eliminate any that are too broad, too narrow, or are possible solutions rather than problem descriptions. You might cull some relevant elements from otherwise unsuitable sentences to incorporate in the final topic sentence or description.

3. Choose the best and **revise** until you get a topic sentence that you agree captures the essence of the problem. Phrases like "because of" or "due to," or verbs like "implement," are red flags that indicate you're jumping ahead and speculating about causes and/or solutions. They don't belong in the problem description.

4. Write the rest of the problem description. Be as explicit as possible about what is included in the problem and, if necessary to avoid confusion, what you will not address as part of *this* project. Check your facts to be sure the description is accurate.

5. Sanity check the description to make sure, given what you know so far, that you've accurately described the problem you intend to solve. Read it yourselves, forgetting everything you know about the situation

> It isn't that they can't see the solution.
> It is that they can't see the problem.
> — G. K. Chesterton

that isn't written on the page. If you didn't already know, could you tell from just reading the description what problem you're going to solve?

Then get someone else, perhaps a colleague somewhat removed from the problem, to read it. Listen carefully to what questions they ask or where they get confused. Listen to yourself when you add explanations or answer questions: the things you're saying should probably be in the description.

6. Revise it as many times as you need to get it clear and concise. If necessary, back up and start brainstorming again to get new ideas.

When it's clear and concise, add it to your worksheet and you're ready to go on.

Identify the Sponsor and Analyst

The *sponsor* is the person who, from a management perspective, is ultimately responsible for making sure the problem gets solved. This is the individual who can allocate resources (such as people's time, money, equipment, etc.), remove roadblocks and generally make it possible for the problem solvers to do their job.

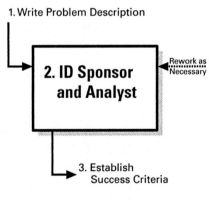

Defining Problems
Process Segment

Although you may have little choice because of your organizational structure or culture, there is often more than one logical candidate to be the sponsor. Think carefully about what characteristics you want the sponsor to have. Typically you want someone who has a major stake in seeing the problem solved, has the power and personality to get things done, has resources to allocate, etc. You may find it helpful to identify all the possible sponsors and "grade" them on the following to help choose the best person overall. Helpful questions to ask are:

> You need a sponsor who can and will champion your work, making it possible for you to succeed.

- Are they in a logical position in the organization? For example, if the problem is related to customer service, the VP of Customer Service is in a more logical position than the VP of Development.
- Will they take the action that is best for the company, even if it is unpopular or risky?
- Are they respected in the company? Will they help win support for your project?
- Do they have or can they get the budget and other resources you'll need?

The more organizations or separate companies involved with the problem, the more critical to have a strong and motivated sponsor. This may be more important than a sponsor who is in the right position in the organization, but is not willing to support your effort vigorously.

The *analyst* is the person responsible for leading the problem solving project. Often someone becomes the analyst because they are handed an assignment by their manager. Sometimes someone takes on the role because they are the first to notice the problem or to feel it is important enough to work on. It is also common for one person to lead the effort until the problem is well enough defined to choose an analyst with experience and skills particularly suited to the problem.

In especially difficult cases where the problem has significant emotion around it, and usually significant business consequences as well, it is best to have an analyst who is outside the situation and whose only role will be to manage and facilitate the problem solving project. Depending on the severity of the situation, "outside" could mean simply uninvolved in the specific situation or it could mean someone completely outside the company.

The sponsor and analyst *must* agree to take on their roles. If you can't get an appropriate sponsor to agree, then either the problem isn't important enough to invest in fixing or you haven't made a persuasive enough case. Whatever the reason, until you have the sponsor's support, at best you are wasting your time and at worst you are risking your career. An analyst who doesn't agree is unlikely to do much work, so the problem will probably stay unsolved.

> HINT: Only one person can be the sponsor. Even though there will probably be several major stakeholders, choose one to be your primary champion.
>
> If you have multiple sponsors, you have no sponsor, and your problem solving effort can easily be derailed by finger pointing or buck passing.
>
> Don't risk it!

Case 1: On-time Shipping Problem

As soon as the group finishes with the problem description, they discuss who the sponsor and analyst should be. You are the analyst, initially because the problem was assigned to you by the President, but also because you are the only person involved who has the skills to lead the *SPP* project.

You are also the sponsor. As Operations Director, it's your job to take care of this type of problem, so you have the authority, resources, etc. The President is certainly interested in the results, but there is no advantage to making him the sponsor. In fact, doing so could undermine the President's efforts to stay out of daily operational issues (and your efforts to keep him out).

Case 2: On-time Software Installation Problem

The team discusses possible sponsors from both BigTel and DAS, but decides that, for a variety of reasons, the BigTel Senior VP would be the best sponsor for his problem. This is a highly political situation, so the team needs a very senior champion. Resources will be required not only from one department, but from several areas within BigTel plus from DAS.

The President of DAS is also involved, and has committed to providing "what it takes." You'll use her to intervene if necessary, but the primary problem is BigTel's. The Senior VP is a no-nonsense individual who will make sure you get what you need—provided that you're demonstrating results. Since you are equally determined to get results, he should be an excellent sponsor.

You are the analyst. The problem was assigned to you and this problem is so important to the company that you would not even consider delegating it.

Do It For Real

Identify the preferred sponsor and analyst for your problem solving project. This is usually fairly obvious, but take enough time to make sure you're choosing the best individuals to support *this* effort. Put their names on the worksheet.

Eventually you will need their agreement to take on the roles, but that can wait until you complete the problem description. If they haven't agreed yet, indicate the assignment is tentative on your worksheet.

Establish Success Criteria

How will you know when the problem is solved? The success criteria answer that question in measurable terms. You and everyone else involved will feel much more confident that a particular problem won't bite you again when you have measurements to prove exactly what effect your solution has.

Characteristics of Good Success Criteria

To be useful, success criteria must be simple in concept and connected so clearly to the problem that you can remember them easily. As with the description, somebody who doesn't already know about the problem should be able to read your success criteria and understand them.

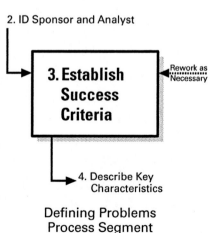

2. ID Sponsor and Analyst

3. Establish Success Criteria

Rework as Necessary

4. Describe Key Characteristics

Defining Problems Process Segment

Each problem will probably have several factors that determine when it is successfully solved. Usually you need to cover two aspects of the problem:

- **Accuracy**, which measures if your solution is correct, i.e., gets the results you want, and,
- **Timeliness**, which measures whether you solved the problem quickly enough.

Both are necessary: a solution that gets 100% accuracy may be worthless if it takes a year to implement, while a solution that is available next week may be worthless if it still allows too many errors.

Once you've figured out what the general factors are for your problem, you need to express them as success criteria. The SMARTI acronym is your checklist to make sure you build your success criteria into a useful form. Each criterion must have the following characteristics:

Specific. Point to the particular problem as precisely as possible.

Measurable. You must be able to tell objectively, i.e., by measuring, whether you've met the criterion or not.

Appropriate. Be sure that whatever you measure will indicate success in solving *this* problem. Metrics that are very broad such as overall revenue growth are usually useless for confirming that a particular problem is solved.

Reasonable. You must have reasonable expectation that you can actually achieve the numbers you agree to. Do you believe you can get the resources (people, time, money/equipment) you need to solve the problem as defined by your success criteria? You don't know yet how you'll solve it, but you should have some sense of how big and messy it is. Use your gut-level assessment. For example, if it will take you full-time work for a week just to analyze the problem and you have other responsibilities, don't promise a total solution within a week.

Time-bound. When will the goal be achieved—a week, month, or year? A 10% improvement in a week is a lot different from a 10% improvement in a year. Start with a gut-level assessment, and refine it later as you learn more.

Important. Only measure characteristics of the problem that matter, i.e., truly measure success. Don't get caught in the trap of measuring something simply because you can.

The objective in setting success criteria is to find the *minimum* necessary to solve the problem. This is completely opposite to the way we usually set goals. The objective in problem solving is to do everything necessary to solve the problem, but nothing extra.

Success criteria are the measurements that will prove the problem is really solved. These may include metrics that have never been reported before, or even require data that has not been collected. As a later part of your problem solving project, you will set up a procedure to collect and report these measurements. Don't let novelty or conservatism stop you from using the right metrics to measure success.

It is usually more useful to express measurements as a rate rather than as an absolute number. For example, rather than using just the number of late shipments, use the number of late shipments as a percent of the total number of shipments. How bad 30 late shipments are depends on whether it's 30 late shipments out of 100 (30% late rate) or 30 late shipments out of 1000 (3% late rate). For many problems, simple rate measurements such as percentage are completely adequate, but you may want to get help from a statistician to be sure your success criteria are telling you what you think they are.

It's very tempting to add in general improvements that are good things to do, but aren't really necessary to solve the problem. Resist the temptation. The work to do those things will distract you from solving the problem, slow you down and may even cause you to fail at solving the problem.

HINT: Everything necessary, nothing extraneous. Use success criteria to make sure you'll solve the problem completely, but won't get sidetracked into doing other things that won't help make *this* problem go away.

HINT: Ask yourself: What will be different when we finish? How will we know?

Case 1: On-time Shipping Problem

The team starts defining the success criteria by building a framework that expresses what you want before worrying about the specific numbers. You write the following, taken quite directly from the description, on the whiteboard to get the discussion started:

xx% of shipments will be on time, complete and correct by ??

The team first addresses the question of whether a successful solution requires that 100% of shipments be on time. You decide that, although 100% would be desirable, reaching that ideal isn't necessary to regard the current problem as solved. You decide 90% is an appropriate standard for your situation. The success criteria now read:

> *90% of shipments will be on time, complete and correct by ??*

Next the team discusses how to define "on time." First you decide the clock should start when the shipment leaves CRF's loading dock, i.e., you choose to eliminate any issues with shippers or at customer sites from the scope of the problem, at least for the initial project. You can reconsider this later if evidence indicates a need.

You also decide that the standard should be the date originally given to the customer. However, to accommodate last minute customer changes you add a rework requirement. You decide 5% will allow some room for last minute adjustments, but basically "on time" means shipments must be complete and correct the first time as well as shipped when promised.

Finally, you tackle the time-bound requirement to make the criteria SMARTI. Before setting this, you check and find that the current on-time ship rate is only 48%. Since it's November now, and current performance is so bad, you decide to use a phased approach that will require higher performance each month until reaching the 90% requirement by April 1. The final success criteria on your worksheet look like this:

- - - - - - - - - - - - - - - - - - - *(form continues)* - - - - - - - - - - - - - - - - - - -

Success Criteria

90% of shipments will be on time and complete, with less than 5% rework, by April 1. "On time" means the entire shipment leaves our loading dock on the date promised to the customer.

By the end of:

Dec., 60% of shipments will meet the standard.

Jan., 70%

Feb., 80%

Mar., 90%

- *(form continues)* -

These success criteria are SMARTI. The percentages are *specific* and *measurable.* Measuring on-time shipping rate is certainly *appropriate* for a problem with missing promised ship dates. The improvement schedule establishes the *timing* and also sets the expectation that, although the 90% level can't be achieved instantly, measurable improvement will occur within a month of when the problem solving project is initiated.

Although you have to know the company situation to be sure, spreading the improvement goals over four months makes the criteria *reasonable* with available resources. The criteria specify improvement in the on-time rate. This is exactly the problem, so the criteria measure what is *important.*

Case 2: On-time Software Installation Problem

The team starts by building a framework:
xx% of installations result in systems back in production on time, beginning ??

When the Senior VP gave you the assignment, he stated that you were to make sure such a fiasco never happened again. Based on that, the team quickly decides 100% is the appropriate number and that it had to be achieved by the next installation. The success criteria now read:

100% of attempted installations result in sys-
tems back in production at 6:00 A.M., begin-
ning with the next installation after this
worksheet is signed.

You use the worksheet sign-off date because it will be a firm, measurable date. Simply saying "next installation" could leave room for argument about exactly when that is.

Then the team discusses how to make the whole thing specific and eliminate any weasel room (previous experience has taught you that any loopholes will be taken advantage of). After trying various combinations and arguing over what is really required, the team agrees to the following success criteria:

- *(form continues)* -

Success Criteria

100% of attempted installations result in systems back in production (i.e., every function is available at 100% of workstations) at 6:00 A.M., beginning with the next installation after this worksheet is signed.

- *(form continues)* -

The team then verifies that the success criteria are SMARTI and further tests them by identifying the possible installation scenarios and assuring the success criteria will measure success or failure correctly. You identify the following possibilities:

- The new software is installed, everything works, and the systems are back in production at 6:00 A.M. This is the best situation: the goal of the new installation is achieved and the installation problem did not occur. The problem success criteria are met.

- The new software has problems, so all functions could not be available at 6:00 A.M. The old software is reinstalled and the system is available at 6:00 A.M., though running the old software. Although the goal of the new installation was not met, the installation problem did not occur. The problem success criteria are met. This situation is not desirable, but addressing that is a different problem.
- The system is not back up at 6:00 A.M., using either the new or the old software. This is exactly the situation that triggered this *SPP* project. If this happens again, the success criteria are not met and the problem is clearly not solved.

Do It For Real

It's time to start developing the success criteria for your own problem.

1. Build the framework. Without worrying about the specific numbers, brainstorm *what* you can measure that will reflect when your problem is solved. Get agreement to a basic statement.

2. Refine the framework. Make sure all aspects of the problem are covered, clarifying anything ambiguous. Watch out for general words like "every," "most," "some" or "all." If that's what you mean, use a specific measurement such as 100% of whatever it is. If you don't really mean it, then replace them with a clearer statement that explains exactly what is included.

3. Cross-check to make sure the problem description and the success criteria match. If you achieve the success criteria and nothing more, will the entire problem be solved? If you truly limit yourself to doing the minimum necessary to achieve the success criteria, will anything important be missed? Is there anything in the success criteria that is not required to solve the problem as described?

Fix any mismatches by adjusting the description or the success criteria, whichever is appropriate for your situation. Collect any additional information you need to be sure you've got it right.

4. Sanity check and **revise.** Reread the description. Are your success criteria logical and do you believe that when you achieve the criteria, the problem will be solved? Make sure the success criteria meet SMARTI. When you're happy with them, add them to your worksheet.

Getting good success criteria is often the most difficult part of defining the problem, but you have to do it to be sure you really do solve the problem and can prove it.

Describe Key Characteristics

Key characteristics are important bits of information that you'll need to know to understand the problem completely and to put together a project to solve it. Usually the following items are sufficient:

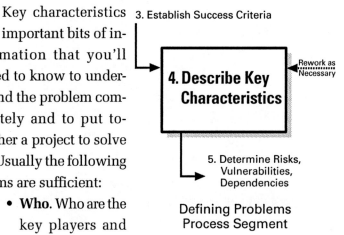

3. Establish Success Criteria

4. Describe Key Characteristics

Rework as Necessary

5. Determine Risks, Vulnerabilities, Dependencies

Defining Problems
Process Segment

- **Who.** Who are the key players and

what is each person's role relative to the problem? Include the people who will be members of the problem solving team, major stakeholders, technical experts who may act as advisors and anyone else who will participate in the problem solving effort in some way. Describe what their involvement will be.

- **Where.** What is the geographic scope of the problem, e.g., confined to one customer site, two manufacturing facilities, worldwide? This information will help you anticipate logistical and possible cultural problems that could affect resource requirements and how quickly you can solve the problem.
- **When.** What is the time-frame of the problem? Is it a single occurrence on a specific date or is it multiple occurrences over a period of time? This information helps you understand the scope of the problem. As usual, you may have to do some research to find out the facts.

Case 1: On-time Shipping Problem

A short discussion confirms the key characteristics. The team decides you have everyone necessary in the room. You consider bringing in the buyer who works with your suppliers and perhaps a representative from sales, but decide to wait until after you understand the problem better to see if that is necessary.

"Where" is simple to answer since CRF is a small company with one factory. "When" is also known to the people in the room, so additional investigation is not needed to find out.

As a result, the Key Characteristics section of the worksheet shows:

- - - - - - - - - - - - - - - - - - - *(form continues)* - - - - - - - - - - - - - - - - - - -

Key Characteristics

Who (key players)

Ops Director, Production Team.

Where

Factory-wide

When

Regular occurrence, getting worse at least over the past six months

- - - - - - - - - - - - - - - - - - - *(form continues)* - - - - - - - - - - - - - - - - - - -

Case 2: On-time Software Installation Problem

As is typical, completing the Key Characteristics is straightforward for this team as well. You identified the key players when you set up the problem solving team. A quick discussion confirms that the group agrees you have the right people. The problem clearly includes all the data centers—five sites located in four states.

Everyone knows the date of the most recent incident, the one that sparked forming the problem solving team. Everyone also knows that the problems had been ongoing for the past year, which was when the implementation phase of the DAS systems began. Your Key Characteristics section looks like this:

- - - - - - - - - - - - - - - - - - - *(form continues)* - - - - - - - - - - - - - - - - - - -

Key Characteristics

Who (key players)

Ops. Managers from each site, Tech. support engineers responsible for installs from both BigTel and DAS.

Where

5 sites in 4 states

When

Worst occurrence: 3/25. Ongoing problem for past year.

- - - - - - - - - - - - - - - - - - - *(form continues)* - - - - - - - - - - - - - - - - - - -

Do It For Real

If the problem description is clear, this section is usually very straightforward.

Complete the *key characteristics* section of your problem worksheet. If your team was formed before you started the *SPP* process, this is a good time to modify the team membership if appropriate. Do you have everybody on the team who is needed to participate in the complete problem solving effort and nobody who isn't?

With the key characteristics described, you're ready to look at some considerations outside the problem itself.

> HINT: People who only need to know what's going on can be informed more efficiently in ways other than having them on the team.

Determine Risks, Vulnerabilities and Dependencies

Identifying risks, vulnerabilities and dependencies is what keeps you from falling into the trap of assuming everything will go right.

4. Describe Key Characteristics

```
┌─────────────────────┐
│ 5. Determine         │  ◀── Rework as
│    Risks,            │      Necessary
│    Vulnerabilities,  │
│    Dependencies      │
└─────────────────────┘
           │
           ▼
   6. Complete the
      Problem Worksheet
```

Defining Problems
Process Segment

- **Risks** are the consequences to your business of not solving the problem. What will happen if you decide not to solve the problem or your problem solving effort fails? If the answer is "not much," maybe the problem isn't important enough to solve.

How big the consequences are tells you something about how much effort should go into the entire project. Usually you only need to lay out the general risks at this point. However, if there is debate about how important the problem is, you should get specific now.

It is often useful to express the size of the risk in financial terms—it helps executives understand how serious the problem really is. The risks explain why you should solve the problem.

- **Vulnerabilities** are all the things that could prevent your problem solving project from succeeding, i.e., could stop you from solving the problem. The bigger the risks, the more important to identify the vulnerabilities.

- **Dependencies** are other people and projects that depend on you solving your problem, or that you are dependent on. You'll need to communicate regularly with the people involved to make sure

HINT: Ask yourself: "What could possibly go wrong?" If something can go wrong, it will. Your job is to make sure nothing important can go wrong.

Knowing the *risks* helps you demonstrate the importance of solving the problem.

Knowing the *vulnerabilities* allows you to make appropriate contingency plans.

Knowing the *dependencies* helps you avoid surprises and enables you to coordinate properly with other projects.

you don't get or provide nasty surprises down the road.

Case 1: On-time Shipping Problem

You lead the team through a standard brainstorming session, starting with risks. Since the problem was assigned to you by the President, you decide a general statement is sufficient. After agreeing on a list of risks, you evaluate the vulnerabilities and dependencies. You put the final list on your worksheet:

- *(form continues)* -

Risks and Vulnerabilities

Risks

Losing existing and potential new customers. Ongoing unnecessary expense of rework, extra shipping, etc.

Vulnerabilities

Priority changes may divert attention from this project. Time available is limited. Staff turnover.

Dependencies

The ongoing project to reduce cycle time from order receipt to final shipment.

- *(end of form)* -

Case 2: On-time Software Installation Problem

As in the On-time Shipping Case, the importance of the problem is well recognized, so the team decides a general statement of risks is sufficient. There is a little debate about whether to include the risk to the executives' bonuses in the list, but the team decides to include it because it is a likely possibility if the problem isn't solved and one that obviously matters to your bosses.

Everyone realizes there is a real vulnerability with getting the Operations Manager from Site A to cooperate. History suggests there might be difficulty, plus that individual isn't present at the meeting, indicating this is already happening. However, there is considerable discussion regarding whether listing it on the worksheet will help or aggravate the situation.

The group finally agrees it is important to be honest, and to deal with such concerns directly. You also agree you'll remove it from the draft so it won't be seen by senior management if, after you talk about the situation with him, he begins to participate fully.

Here is the Risks and Vulnerabilities section of the problem worksheet before the discussion with the Operations Manager for Site A:

- *(form continues)* -

Risks and Vulnerabilities

Risks

BigTel may not get rate increase (or execs their bonuses) if this problem is not solved quickly. DAS may lose BigTel as a customer. As the business is deregulated, BigTel will be unable to compete if this problem isn't solved: the problem threatens BigTel's long-term viability as a company.

Vulnerabilities

Ops. Mgr. from Site A may refuse to participate. Funding is not yet allocated for this project.

Dependencies

DAS has just started an initiative to improve software quality—need to coordinate with that team.

- *(end of form)* -

Do It For Real

Identify the risks, vulnerabilities and dependencies for your own problem.

1. Brainstorm everything you can think of for each category. Sometimes it's not clear whether something is a vulnerability or a dependency. This isn't important, so just put it wherever is most logical to you. The important thing is to identify everything that could affect your ability to meet your success criteria.

2. Discuss and **revise** the list. Eliminate duplicates and anything so remote that it really isn't worth considering. If you're not sure, keep it in.

Complete the Problem Worksheet

You've now got a worksheet that has all the sections filled in. The last step in defining the problem is to make sure it's complete and correct.

Start by cross-checking the entire worksheet for completeness and consistency. Use the *SPP Checklist* in the Appendix to help make sure you cover everything. Confirm that the problem description is based on facts.

5. Determine Risks, Vulnerabilities, Dependencies

Rework as Necessary

6. Complete the Problem Worksheet

Defining Problems Process Segment

Be especially careful that the problem description and the success criteria match. Compare them point by point. Everything in the problem description should be measured by the success criteria. Everything in the success criteria should measure some

> Do you understand what the problem is and personally believe it is worth solving? If not, either drop the problem or redefine it until you do.

aspect of the problem presented in the problem description. If they don't match, change them as necessary until they do and you believe you have "everything necessary, nothing extraneous."

The last step before you proceed to the next chapter is to check your success criteria with real data. This accomplishes two things:

1. Verifies that you can actually use the success criteria that you've defined. There are two questions you need to answer:

- Can you actually collect and report the data you need, and
- Does it tell you what you thought it would?

2. Establishes baselines. Measuring exactly where your performance is before you start taking corrective actions accomplishes several key things:

- Confirms that there really is a problem, and
- Sanity checks the performance levels you've defined as "success" and the time frame. Are they reasonable?

If necessary, revise your success criteria.

Case 1: On-time Shipping Problem

Cross-checking the worksheet confirms that the team agrees it describes the problem properly. If you hadn't done it already, you would check now to establish your baseline: current performance for on-time shipping is 48%.

Knowing this number confirms both that you can collect the measurement and that it tells you what you want to know about performance (no wonder customers are complaining!). The final worksheet, unless something happens later to cause changes, looks like this:

Solving Problems Permanently^{SM}
Problem Worksheet

Problem Description

Customers are complaining that shipments are frequently late, incomplete or simply incorrect. They are unhappy as these delays are expensive and impact their ability to serve their customers.

On-time, correct shipments are necessary, but CRF must remain flexible to accommodate last-minute customer changes and special requirements. Handling returns and redoing incorrect orders is also expensive for CRF.

Sponsor

Operations Director

Analyst

Operations Director

Success Criteria

90% of shipments will be on time and complete, with less than 5% rework, by April 1. "On time" means the entire shipment leaves our loading dock on the date promised to the customer.

By the end of:

Dec., 60% of shipments will meet the standard.

Jan., 70%

Feb., 80%

Mar., 90%

Key Characteristics

Who (key players)

Ops Director, Production Team.

Where

Factory-wide

When

Regular occurrence, getting worse at least over the past six months

Risks and Vulnerabilities

Risks

Losing existing and potential new customers. Ongoing unnecessary expense of rework, extra shipping, etc.

Vulnerabilities

Priority changes may divert attention from this project. Time available is limited. Staff turnover.

Dependencies

The ongoing project to reduce cycle time from order receipt to final shipment.

Case 2: On-time Software Installation Problem

You and the team cross-check the worksheet, find that the success criteria do indeed match the description, and confirm you are satisfied that the worksheet provides a good basis to proceed with your problem solving effort. Since the success criteria result in a simple yes/no answer, it is easy to verify that it can be determined. The final worksheet looks like this:

Solving Problems Permanently*SM*
Problem Worksheet

Problem Description

Installation of new releases is rarely completed in the scheduled time. Both operators and customers get angry and frustrated when the system is not available as planned. BigTel loses money and credibility.

Installation includes all software (application, operating system) on all equipment including mainframes, networking equipment and workstations. "Completed" means fully back in production such that operators can perform their normal duties.

Sponsor

Senior VP of Operator Services

Analyst

You

Success Criteria

100% of attempted installations result in systems back in production (i.e., every function is available at 100% of workstations) at 6:00 A.M., beginning with the next installation after this worksheet is signed.

Key Characteristics

Who (key players)

Ops. Managers from each site, Tech. support engineers responsible for installs from both BigTel and DAS.

Where

5 sites in 4 states

When

Worst occurrence: 3/25. Ongoing problem for past year.

Risks and Vulnerabilities

Risks

BigTel may not get rate increase (or execs their bonuses) if this problem is not solved quickly. DAS may lose BigTel as a customer. As the business is deregulated, BigTel will be unable to compete if this problem isn't solved: the problem threatens BigTel's long-term viability as a company.

Vulnerabilities

Ops. Mgr. from Site A may refuse to participate. Funding is not yet allocated for this project.

Dependencies

DAS has just started an initiative to improve software quality—need to coordinate with that team.

Do It For Real

Now is the time to cross-check your own problem worksheet.

1. Check individual sections of the worksheet using the *SPP Checklist* in the Appendix. If you can't answer "yes" to each item, revise the section until you can.

2. Cross-check the sections with each other. Be sure the success criteria cover *everything necessary, nothing extraneous* when compared to the written description. Are the risks, vulnerabilities and dependencies specific to *this* problem as described in the problem description?

3. Verify with data. Establish your baselines and make sure the metrics really will tell you when the problem is solved. If necessary, adjust the success criteria. At this point, collect the data any way you can. You'll establish regular procedures and design your reports in the next step.

4. Revise the worksheet until everything matches, you believe it's complete and correct, and you know that your success criteria work.

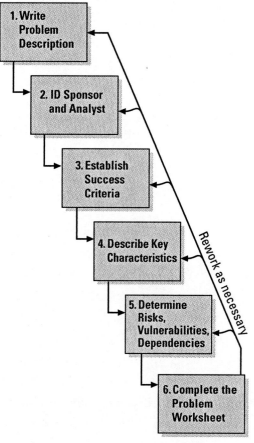

Defining Problems Process Flow

If you've completed the above steps, your problem is defined and you're ready to go on.

Now you're ready to decide whether your problem is suitable for *SPP* and if it is, organize your problem solving project. By defining it carefully, you've finished the hardest and most important part of solving your problem.

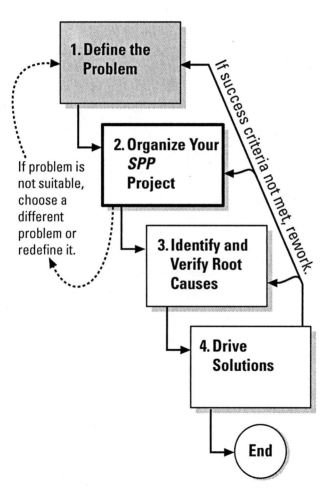

Solving Problems Permanently[SM] Process Flow

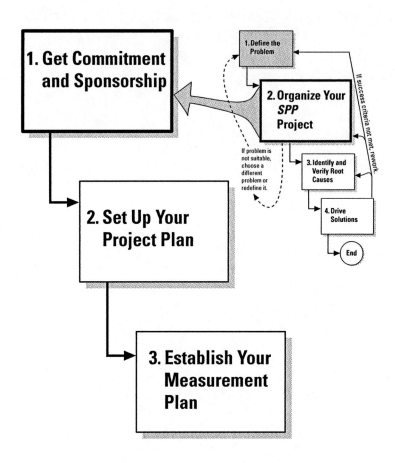

Organizing Your Project Process Flow

Organize Your *Solving Problems Permanently*^{SM} Project

Y ou now have a completed problem worksheet for the problem you're planning to solve. "Completed" at this point means

> HINT: You're still not ready to investigate, or even think about, how you will solve your problem!

1. You think it describes the problem completely and accurately, and

2. You are satisfied that everyone who reads it will understand correctly what will be different when you finish solving the problem.

If you have a team working with you, they agree. Now you will use the problem statement to answer some key questions that will determine whether you can (and should) go ahead and solve the problem. The steps are shown in the Organizing Your Project Process Flow diagram.

Get Commitment and Sponsorship

Analyzing and solving messy problems is a lot of work, so make sure it's worth it. Decide explicitly whether to proceed by answering the following questions:

```
┌─────────────────────┐
│ 1. Get Commitment   │
│    and Sponsorship  │
└─────────────────────┘
        │
        └──────▶ 2. Set Up Your
                    Project Plan
```

Organizing Your Project Process Segment

- Is it **important**? Be sure the impact of the problem is high enough to justify investing the resources it will take to fix it. Look especially carefully at the risks section of your worksheet. How bad will it be if you don't fix the problem? If it is not clear to you and everyone else involved whether you should go ahead, you need to do more work.

Quantify the cost of the problem as realistically as you can. Include lost opportunity costs as well

> *We have to learn to distinguish those things that are truly important from those that are merely urgent.*
> — Jerry D. Campbell
>
> Just because a problem is there does not mean you have to fix it.

as real expenses such as staff time to deal with the problem, travel expenses, etc. Revise your problem worksheet to include this information. Then guesstimate what it will cost to analyze and fix it.

If it will cost more to fix than to live with the problem, or if the numbers are even close, perhaps your resources (time, people, money) are better spent on other projects. On the other hand, if you can demonstrate that the cost of the problem is much higher than the cost of solving it, using estimates based on reasonable assumptions, it should be relatively easy to get the resources you need.

- Is the problem a **mess**? Reread your problem statement, especially the problem description and the key characteristics. If it's a mess, use *SPP*.
- Is it **well defined** and **small enough** to be manageable? Reread the problem description and the success criteria. The scope of your work must be clear before you can begin analyzing the problem.

  If the mess is so big you can't see the boundaries, you need to find ways of breaking it up into smaller chunks. Solve part of the problem at a time. For example, if it involves a multi-vendor network, perhaps you can limit the initial effort to the products of one or two vendors or start with two key sites. Look at the larger environment after you understand the smaller.

- Can you get the necessary **commitment** to do the project, or at least get started? If you haven't already done it, now is the time to be sure the sponsor accepts the job. If nobody with the power to be effective is willing to be the sponsor, your chances of success are remote.

The sponsor is the person who can allocate re-sources, remove obstacles, etc. If you can't convince the sponsor to care, you should spend your time on something else. Getting commitment is usually rather easy if the problem is truly significant and you've made the case on the problem statement, especially the assessment of risks.

You must also be sure that all the other key play-ers accept the problem statement and agree to un-dertake their roles. For example, if you've identified somebody as a member of the problem solving team, be sure they are willing and avail-able to take the assignment. If they aren't, they will never come to team meetings or do any work. Of course, you can and should try to persuade them, get their assignments changed, etc., if they are es-sential to your problem solving effort.

You always want explicit approval to proceed. Depending on the size of the problem and how your company works, verbal approval may be enough or you may want a formal sign-off. People tend to take things more seriously when they sign them, and you then have a written record of your agreement in case there is confusion later.

Whether signed or not, your agreed-to problem statement acts like a contract between you and the problem sponsor. You're both agreeing to exactly what results you require and how your perfor-mance will be measured. This may seem scary, but it's a lot safer than letting the boss decide after the fact whether you've done the right thing.

Case 1: On-time Shipping Problem

By the time you finish with the worksheet, you and your team are not only convinced the problem needs solving (though in this case you didn't need the worksheet to tell you that), but also that you have laid out success criteria that define an adequate solution and are achievable. Although faster achievement would be nice, you are convinced you can't guarantee faster results.

Since you are both the analyst and the sponsor, you don't have to work too hard to get your own agreement. Nevertheless, you make sure to review the worksheet with the President since he is obviously a key stakeholder.

Case 2: On-time Software Installation Problem

Although you and your team share some concern about achieving the high standard required by the success criteria, you all realize that nothing less will be acceptable and you'd better find a way to do it or find new jobs. The Senior VP readily agrees that the worksheet is an accurate description and is relieved to see you taking a systematic approach to dealing with it. Although she is not the sponsor, you also review the worksheet with the President of DAS to make sure she understands what is required and will support her people in helping achieve success.

Do It For Real

Before proceeding, make sure your problem is suitable for using *SPP* and that you are ready to proceed.

The steps are:

1. **Verify** that you personally believe the problem is worth solving and that you can meet the success criteria. If you don't believe it yourself, either drop it (for example, if it isn't important enough) or go back to your problem statement and rework it until you do believe it.

2. **Get commitment** from the sponsor and other key players. Explain to each person what the problem is, why it's important and what you need from them to be successful. Make sure each agrees to undertake their role. If appropriate, get signatures.

Once you have agreement from everyone, you can proceed to set up your project and solve the problem. If a key player does not agree, you'll have to address their objections before you can proceed.

Set Up Your Project Plan

Solving a complicated problem is a project and must be treated that way to make sure you can keep up with all the pieces. As with any project, you'll need to identify tasks, make and adjust assignments, and keep track of what is due when. We'll cover some of the basics here. If you need more help, there are many books and seminars on project management.

1. Get Commitment and Sponsorship

2. Set Up Your Project Plan

3. Establish Your Measurement Plan

Organizing Your Project Process Segment

Start Your Task List

The first step is to start your project task list. This will be your tool to keep track of everything that's going on in

> HINT: Orient tasks to deliverables. Each task should result in something tangible. This will help you make sure the tasks actually accomplish something.

your project. Every time you think of something that needs to be done, put it on your task list. That way, you don't have to worry about forgetting important details.

For most problems, a simple table maintained using your favorite wordprocessor or spreadsheet is sufficient. You can use the template shown below.

Task	Completion Criteria	Owner	Due Date
Project Management			
Measurement Plan			
Communication Plan			
Contingency Plans: [one plan for each vulnerability you are addressing]			
Action Plans: [one plan for each root cause you are addressing]			

Task List Template

The task list is a working document: add, change and delete tasks as you go so that the list is always up to date. Always assign a task owner, due date and completion criteria for every task.

The task owner is the individual responsible for making sure the task gets done, whether directly by doing the work personally or indirectly by assigning it to someone else. As always, the owner must agree to accept the responsibility. If you're the analyst, it's your job to make sure tasks get assigned to willing owners with the necessary skills.

The completion criteria are success criteria for a task. They tell you objectively that the task has been completed properly. For example, suppose someone is assigned the task to design the success criteria reports that you will use to track how effective your solution is. Is the task complete when the report designer says it is or must the reports meet some other standard such as being accepted by the team?

> HINT: Use completion criteria to avoid misunderstandings and delays.

Be sure to group tasks that are related and note dependencies. You can note these in the task description or, if you prefer, add a column for them. If your project involves lots of activities that are dependent on each other, it may be worth using project management software to help keep track of it all.

It is useful to divide your task list into sections for the basic categories of tasks. For example, group together the tasks necessary to manage your project. Similarly, group the tasks for your measurement plan, communication plan, contingency plans and the action plans that will eliminate the causes you select. Add these sections as you get to them.

Case 1: On-time Shipping Problem

You start the task list on a flip chart in the team meeting, listing tasks as you go. At the end of the meeting, you go back through the list determining completion criteria, assigning owners and setting due dates. Part of the task list, just after the problem statement is approved, might look like this.

Task	Completion Criteria	Owner	Due Date
Project Management Develop project schedule	1st version accepted by team	Ops. Dir.	11/7 & weekly
Review work-sheet with President	He accepts it	Ops. Dir.	11/5
Measurement Plan Design success criteria reports	Reports approved by team and by Pres.	Production Supervisor	11/7
Set up measure-ment procedures	Report completed using new procedures	Production Supervisor	11/14

On-time Shipping Problem: Initial Task List

The task list can be started by listing tasks directly from the steps in *SPP*, as is done here with the steps in the measurement plan. You will add general tasks at first, breaking them down into more detailed tasks as you figure out exactly what you need for your particular situation.

Case 2: On-time Software Installation Problem

With a problem as big and urgent as this one, it is useful to start the task list as soon as the assignment is made. This helps you move more quickly and avoid mistakes as you get this major effort underway. Part of an initial task list, begun before the problem statement is approved, might look like this. Today is 4/1, and your name is "Yu."

Task	Completion Criteria	Owner	Due Date
Project Management Identify team members & get buy-in from them and their managers	everybody agrees	Yu	4/2
Schedule team meeting	conf. room booked, agenda distributed	Yu	4/2
Measurement Plan Design success criteria reports	Reports approved by team	Ops. Mgr. Site B	2nd mtg.
Communication Plan Set up email distribution list	List created	Yu	4/2
Write and send status report	1st report sent	Yu	4/5 and weekly on Fridays
Contingency Plan: Ops. Mgr. from Site A participation Hold special mtg. w/ Site A Ops Mgr. to encourage, address concerns	Mtg. held, Ops. Mgr. commits to support effort	Yu	4/3

On-time Software Installation Problem: Initial Task List

At this point, the project has really just been initiated. The first tasks are all focused on getting the team together, explaining individually to team members and their managers what this effort is about and asking for their participation. One of the vulnerabilities listed on the problem worksheet is that the Operations Manager from Site A may refuse to participate. To avoid the kind of difficulties this person has caused in the past, you're setting up a special meeting to present the project, reassure the manager that it is not a personal attack, etc.

Set Up the Project Schedule

Next lay out a project schedule. Your success criteria should tell you when the problem solution is due. Work backwards from there to figure out when you'll have to complete the steps of the *SPP* process. Identify any other key milestones that will help you keep your *SPP* project on track. For example, you might want to set up one or more formal progress reports for the sponsor and key stakeholders. Add the appropriate tasks to your task list. For example, a progress report might require tasks to write the report, to write a cover memo and to distribute the report.

Estimate Resources and Get Them Allocated

Estimate the resources you'll require. You've already checked with the key players, but are there other people whose help you will need? Will you need money for travel, special equipment, or anything else? Will you need use of existing equipment, exclusive use of a conference room, or access to any other special resources? If yes, now is the time to figure out what you need and get it allocated. Again, use your task list to identify and track the steps necessary to do it. You may need to adjust the schedule and possibly your success criteria if you cannot get certain resources.

Do It For Real

Set up the project plan for your problem using the Task List Template in the Appendix.

1. Start your **task list.** Write down everything you can think of that needs to be done or may need to be done to get your *SPP* project started. Group together the small tasks that make up a larger one. Assign tentative owners, due dates and completion criteria. Mark everything tentative with a question mark until you confirm it so you can tell at a glance what is committed.

Consider what you need to do to start working on the problem. The steps of the *SPP* process described in this book provide a high-level list or outline of the tasks you'll need. Of course, you'll need to fill in the specific tasks for your problem. Initially many of your tasks will involve collecting information.

2. Establish your **communication plan.** Specify who needs what information about your problem solving effort, when they need it and how you are going to provide it. Add tasks to your task list to implement these decisions.

3. Develop contingency plans. Go back to the vulnerabilities and dependencies on your problem statement.

Add tasks to your task list to eliminate vulnerabilities or at least limit their impact if they occur. If you don't know yet what to do, set up tasks to develop and implement those contingency plans. Similarly, add appropriate tasks to handle the dependencies.

4. Develop the project **schedule.** Add writing presentations and reports for milestones and other key dates to your task list. Adjust due dates for the tasks you've already identified accordingly.

5. Estimate and **get resources.** Figure out what you'll need, at least for the initial part of the project and get them allocated. Put the tasks to do it on your task list. Then do them. Check that your schedule is still correct, adjusting if necessary.

6. Cross-check with your problem definition to make sure everything is still aligned. Everything on your task list should contribute to your ability to achieve your success criteria. Make sure nothing extra has crept in. If anything is out of alignment, adjust appropriately.

7. Confirm tentative **assignments.** Do it now for tasks with due dates that are soon. For tasks that are farther out, do it as soon as you're sure the task really needs to be done. Always give the owner as much notice as possible.

8. Update your task list, schedule and resource requirements throughout the life of the project. They are tools to help you make sure everything gets done correctly and on time.

Establish Your Measurement Plan

You will use a success criteria report to show progress as
you go and ultimately, to prove
you have solved the problem.
The success criteria on your
problem statement tell you
what to measure, and you established your baselines when
you verified your worksheet.
Now you can use that informa-

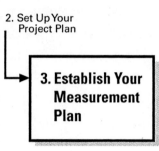

2. Set Up Your Project Plan

3. **Establish Your Measurement Plan**

Organizing Your Project Process Segment

tion to establish the details of exactly how you will gather
the data on an ongoing basis and track your progress.
For example, will you graph a trend over time, present
data in tabular form or what? How often will you update your measurements?

Create your first progress report now, showing all of
your success criteria as you will report them regularly
and at the end of the project. This first report gives your
baseline data. It shows the status of your problem at the
beginning of the project, before you've taken any actions
to improve things.

Case 1: On-time Shipping Problem

The initial measurement report shows your baseline
metrics for all of your success criteria. This problem uses
two key measurements, percent of on-time shipments
and percent rework, so the report will have two charts.

Although CRF has never reported this information
before, the raw data is available. However, it is laborious

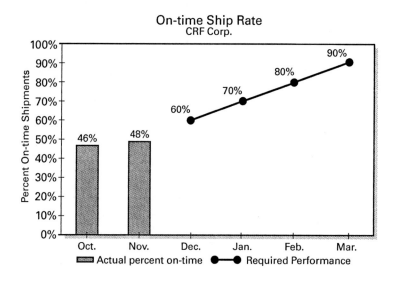

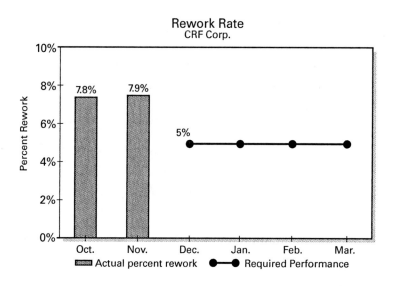

On-time Shipping Problem: Baseline Success Criteria

to pull together after the fact, so the team agrees that the Production Supervisor should create the initial report with only one previous month. If the data had been easier to gather, you would have liked to see a longer history. Of course, you'll track these measurements every month from now on.

The two charts show at a glance how far both the current on-time ship rate and the rework rate are from the required performance. To create the charts, the team had to make a number of decisions about the measurements themselves as well as how to show them.

For example, the team chose to measure rework in hours rather than pieces, expressed as a percent of total hours worked. This data was readily available, and for CRF the primary cost of rework is in labor costs. Measuring by hours is both easy and appropriate in this case. Although these two charts are sufficient to track success criteria, the team will always want to be sure to have detailed backup data available to answer any questions.

Case 2: On-time Software Installation Problem

For this problem, the measurement is very simple. For each installation attempted, either the systems are completely back in production at 6:00 A.M. or they are not. The following shows the initial report with the "final straw" installation that resulted in you getting the assignment to fix it.

Because only a few new installations are normally undertaken in a year, and to emphasize that close is not good enough, the team decided to use a report-card format that

Installation Report Card			
Description	**Date**	**Pass/Fail**	**Comments**
Install v. 3.1.7 DAS soft-ware (bug fixes & new features). Install new disk drives.	3/25	F	Full production 6 hours late. Software not ready until noon; disk drive ready at 8:00 A.M. Action: Yu heading *SPP* project to find out why and fix.

On-time Software Installation Problem:
Baseline Success Criteria

shows a simple pass/fail for each installation. In the case of a failure, detail will be added explaining exactly what went wrong and any corrective actions already taken. Any F's after the one that caused the *SPP* project to be initiated mean the success criteria were not met.

Do It For Real

Set up your measurements for your own problem:

1. Design your success criteria reports. Decide all the details: how you will present the data itself, titles, page numbers, etc. Keep in mind that lots of people will review this data who aren't in the middle of the problem solving project—keep it simple and self-explanatory. Also decide how frequently you will update your report.

2. Implement a procedure for collecting the data and producing the report to meet your design. Depending on your problem, this may be as simple as setting up a tally sheet or it may itself be a complicated project, such as if you need software developed to get information from corporate databases.

3. Update your communication plan. You've already established a basic communication plan, but now that you know how you'll track success criteria you can update it to include your success criteria reports. Decide who needs to know how you are progressing and how you will convey the information. Certainly your team members and the problem sponsor will need this information. Use the opportunity to keep other key stakeholders informed. Make sure tasks to make it happen get assigned and included on your task list.

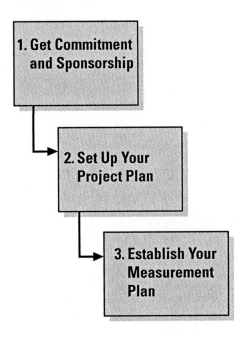

Organizing Your Project Process Flow

If you've done all the steps in this chapter, you've completed the following key milestones in your project. You have

- An approved project to solve an important problem,
- Agreement on exactly what the problem is, including measurements to prove when you're done and to track progress along the way,
- Your first success criteria report completed,
- Tools in place to manage your project: task list, schedule and communication plan, and
- Resources allocated.

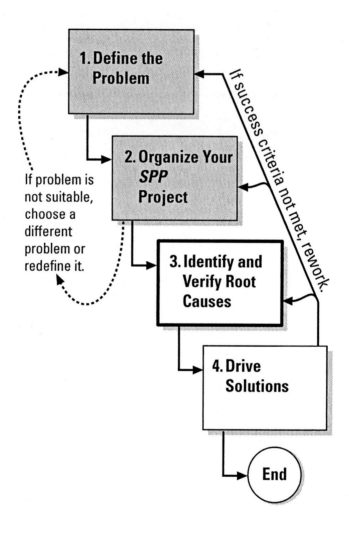

Solving Problems Permanently^{SM} Process Flow

Identify and Verify Root Causes

You now have an approved problem statement that defines your problem, and you're organized to manage your problem solving project. The problem statement tells you *what;* the root cause analysis (RCA) will tell you *why.* You're ready to find out specifically what causes your problem. Only after you know that can you start to consider solutions.

"Stuff" doesn't just happen. Some condition, previous event or prior action causes a problem to occur. In the RCA step of *SPP*, you'll systematically analyze the problem to identify the root causes. Since the problem

> The Root Cause Analysis step tells *why* the problem occurs. If you know that, you can fix the problem permanently.

is a mess, there will usually be multiple causes. When you know the causes, you know where to focus action to eliminate them. Removing the causes prevents the problem from occurring again.

There are many different RCA techniques, each effective for different types of problems and different situations. This book presents only one of them, Ishikawa Analysis, as the core of the RCA step because it is an effective general-purpose method that is relatively quick and easy to use. You can use another method if you prefer, but it should be systematic and aimed at identifying the root causes of your problem.

Invented by Kaoru Ishikawa in 1943, Ishikawa Analysis is also referred to as Cause-and-Effect Analysis or Fishbone Analysis. Regardless of its name, Ishikawa Analysis is a group process that relies on synergy and collective knowledge to develop a comprehensive list of possible root causes. If you've used Ishikawa Analysis before, you'll notice that *SPP* adds some special steps to make it easier and quicker.

What You Get From Ishikawa Analysis

Ishikawa Analysis is a structured but relatively informal RCA technique. It helps you organize a brainstorm session to get a particular result, specifically a diagram that shows categorized groups of possible root causes. You can then verify the causes, set priorities and develop an action plan to eliminate the significant ones.

> *Cause-and-effect diagrams are drawn to clearly illustrate the various causes affecting product quality by sorting out and relating the causes. Therefore, a good cause-and-effect diagram is one that fits the purpose, and there is no definite form.*
>
> —Kaoru Ishikawa

An Ishikawa diagram is very flexible in form, which makes it adaptable to a wide variety of problems. However, the flexibility that makes it powerful also provides a challenge: the basic form is easy to understand, but there are few rules to tell you exactly how to structure the content.

An Ishikawa diagram, as adapted for *SPP*, takes the general form shown below.

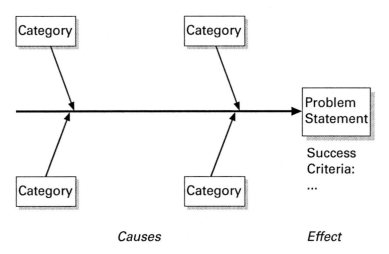

Ishikawa Diagram: General Form

You will create a diagram specifically for your problem that will follow this model. The head of the diagram contains a brief statement of your problem. Usually you can use the topic sentence from your problem description. Below it, list your success criteria, also taken from the problem statement. The body of the diagram shows the causes, successively broken down and organized by category.

Most of the work in an Ishikawa Analysis is done in a single meeting of specially invited participants. As the analyst, you will set up the meeting, invite the participants, and set their expectations about what will happen. The steps to create your Ishikawa diagram and complete the RCA phase of *SPP* are as shown in the Ishikawa Analysis Process Flow.

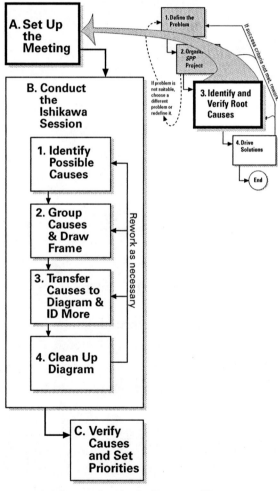

Ishikawa Analysis Process Flow

Set Up the Meeting

Invite the Participants

Ishikawa Analysis is a group process that relies on collective knowledge. To be effective, the group must include everyone who has good knowledge of the problem (or type of problem) and can contribute to understanding it. Normally you will include members of your team plus selected subject matter experts. Subject matter experts are individuals with specific expertise related to the problem.

> **A. Set Up the Meeting**
>
> → B. Conduct the Ishikawa Session
>
> Ishikawa Analysis Process Segment

Large groups are hard to manage and can inhibit participation, so don't invite people who cannot truly contribute to identifying possible

> HINT: Check again—have you included everyone necessary, nobody extraneous?

root causes. You've probably identified the necessary key players in the *Who* section of your problem statement, but ask yourself again if you have "everyone necessary, nobody extraneous."

For an effective session, you must somehow get everyone in a room together at the same time. It is critical that *all* appropriate individuals be present for the session because it is the interaction of the group that brings out key ideas. The session must be face-to-face, which can make scheduling a challenge.

Conference calls and even video conferences do not work well for Ishikawa sessions. Difficult as it is, if it's important to solve the problem, you'll have to get everyone there. Ask the problem sponsor for help adjusting other people's priorities if you need to. Bribery with food, especially chocolate, has also been known to be effective.

Choose a Facilitator

An effective Ishikawa session needs a facilitator to make sure the meeting results in a useful Ishikawa diagram. The facilitator is responsible for keeping the discussion on track, and generally making sure (tactfully) that everyone participates appropriately in the discussion. The facilitator guides the group by

- Providing the method and structure to make the meeting successful,
- Guiding the group from scattered thinking to an organized direction, and
- Insuring that the group creates an Ishikawa diagram that everyone supports.

The analyst will usually be the facilitator, but, depending on the nature of the problem, you may want to use an experienced outside facilitator. It could be someone from another department, or it may need to be someone completely outside the company. Consider using an outside facilitator when:

- The analyst needs to participate actively in the discussion. It is impossible to attend both to the process of running the meeting and to the content of the discussion, especially if the discussion is intense. Everyone who has ideas about what is causing your problem needs to participate in the discussion. Get someone else to facilitate.

- You anticipate a difficult or emotional discussion. Experienced facilitators know how to handle these situations. An outsider can make sure everyone is heard and keep the discussion fair without being perceived as manipulating the discussion.

Practicalities and Logistics

You're asking busy people to give you time. If you use it well, they'll support your work and be happy to help. If you waste their time (or they think you did), you'll have a struggle to get their participation next time. There are some things you can do to help make sure everything goes smoothly.

- Follow good meeting practices. Make sure everyone knows what to expect. Use ground rules to govern group behavior during the meeting and post off-agenda topics on a flip chart (often called a parking lot). Decide how to address the parking lot issues at the end of the meeting, after you complete the planned agenda. There are many resources available on conducting effective meetings if you need help.

- Allow enough time. How long you need depends on the participants in the session as well as the messiness of the problem. Remember to include adequate time for breaks.

As a rule of thumb, start with a half day. Add more time if the participants don't already know each other, are not already familiar with the

problem as defined on your problem
statement, or if the problem is especially complicated.

People will
protest. Be ready
to remind them
about the impor-
tance of the pro-
blem and why
their participa-
tion is necessary.

> HINT: It's better to
> schedule too much
> time than too little.
>
> Nobody will complain if
> you finish early, but
> they'll be angry if you
> keep them late or need
> another meeting.

The time required for a successful Ishikawa session is a small investment compared to the cost of
the problem.

- Use appropriate facilities. The session is long, so
  make sure the room is large enough for people to
  be able to move comfortably and spread out their
  materials. Consider using a location away from
  your participants' offices so there will be fewer
  interruptions.

  You need a very large whiteboard everyone can
  see. The electronic kind that prints what you've
  written can be useful, but they're usually too small.
  An alternative if you don't have a big enough
  whiteboard is to cover a wall with butcher paper.
  It's not as convenient as a large whiteboard, but is
  preferable to a small one.

  Provide food and beverages, but not so much that
  everybody goes to sleep. It's hard to concentrate
  on a discussion when your stomach is growling.

- Note-taking is critical. If possible, have someone attend the meeting just to take notes. They should be familiar with the subject so they'll understand abbreviations and special terms.

   Have the note-taker copy the diagram as you build it since sometimes it's hard to read the board by the end of the session. Transcribe the diagram to a computer immediately, before you forget what you meant, and distribute it to the participants for correction right away.

- Thank the participants at the end of the meeting and again shortly after it. Write thank you notes, possibly with copies to the participants' managers, acknowledging their contributions to solving a problem that is important to your company. Recognize that you asked a lot and appreciate their time and willingness to help.

Do It For Real

Set up your meeting:

1. Decide when and where you want to hold the meeting. Figure out how much time you'll need. Make the necessary arrangements for the facilities.

2. Invite the participants, facilitator if it's not you, and a note taker. Give everyone the problem statement, explain it and what the Ishikawa session is for.

3. Remind everyone about the session shortly before the meeting.

4. Check the room ahead of time. Make sure tables and chairs are arranged properly, you have enough markers, etc. Be sure you know how to adjust the heat/air conditioning.

Conduct the Ishikawa Session

You create your Ishikawa diagram in the session. After introductions, review what the problem is and what the objective of the Ishikawa session is. Then lead the group through the following steps. If you're using an outside facilitator, this is where they take over.

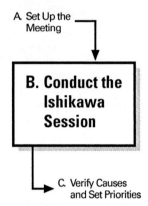

A. Set Up the Meeting

B. Conduct the Ishikawa Session

C. Verify Causes and Set Priorities

Ishikawa Analysis Process Segment

HINT: Start the meeting by explaining (again) what the problem is and that the purpose of the session is to identify possible causes.

The repetition is necessary to get everyone focused properly.

Identify Possible Causes: 1st Pass

Start by reminding everyone that you're looking for anything that could cause the problem to occur. Ask them to think about two questions:
- Why is this problem happening?
- Why are we not achieving the success criteria now—what is in the way?

Give everyone a pad of sticky notes, all the same color and size, and ask everyone to write everything they can think of that might answer those questions on a note.

Put each idea on a separate note, writing just enough to make the idea clear. This should be done very quickly, usually in about ten minutes. The idea is to get possibilities without worrying now about how likely they are. Stop when ideas stop flowing easily.

Group Causes into Categories and Draw Diagram Frame

Next, sort the notes into logical groupings. Have everyone stick their notes on the wall, grouping ideas they think are related by putting the notes physically near each other. Everyone works simultaneously, and no talking is allowed. The facilitator should only intervene if necessary to make sure everyone participates and to remind people not to talk.*

Anyone who thinks they have a more logical grouping should simply move the notes accordingly. You're done when everyone steps back and stops moving notes.

HINT: If the group is larger than 10-12 people, this technique doesn't work well. With a large group, draw the frame directly and make a guess as to appropriate categories. People can use their notes individually as reminders of things to bring up.

HINT: Do not allow categorization by department, company or organization. It's worse than not useful: it will promote finger-pointing and blaming. This is one of the few places the facilitator should overrule the group if necessary.

* This technique is called creating an *affinity diagram.* Although not traditionally used in creating Ishikawa diagrams, it's a useful tool for getting initial thoughts out and for identifying the most natural categories quickly.

Now the facilitator can walk everyone through the notes, eliminating duplicates and clarifying wording. Frequently the same words are used to mean different things. These are not duplicates, so watch out for them. To keep things manageable, combine groups, especially if many of them have only a few causes. Four is a good target number of groups or categories.

Name the groups, using general terms such as Procedures, People, Product, or Tools. These will be the category names on your Ishikawa diagram, though you may certainly change them later. You want general terms that will make it easy to add more causes, but not so general that they get huge. Don't agonize over this now: if a category starts to get too big, you can always divide it later.

Now it's time to start building the Ishikawa diagram itself. Draw the frame on the whiteboard, following the general form given above. Make it as big as you can— you'll need the space. Write the problem in the box at the head of the diagram, and list the success criteria below it. Each category gets a line leading into the main "spine" of the diagram.

Case 1: On-time Shipping Problem

The following shows the whiteboard with sticky notes grouped into categories. The team quickly stuck them on the board and moved them around into the general areas shown. You drew a circle around the ones that were grouped together, and made a guess as to what to label the categories.

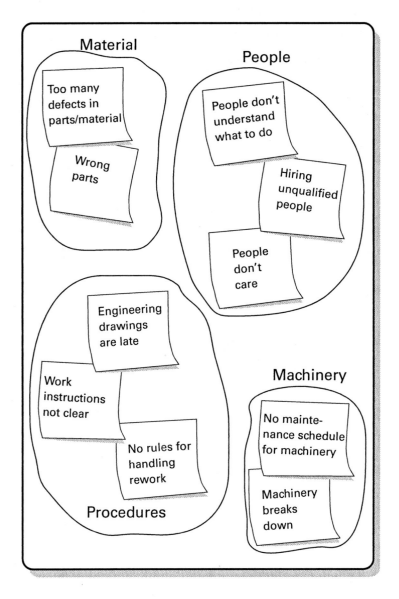

On-time Shipping Problem: Grouped Sticky Notes

When you asked the group what they thought, they agreed this was a good start. (Normally, you'd have many more notes than this, but the idea here is to demonstrate how it's done.)

You then draw the frame, using the category names you've just chosen and the problem statement and success criteria from your worksheet.

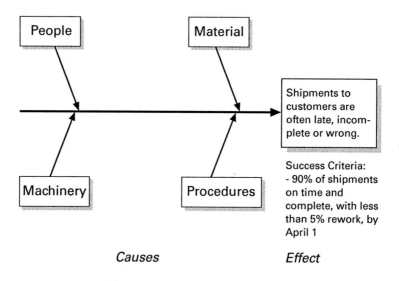

On-time Shipping Problem: Ishikawa Frame

Case 2: On-time Software Installation Problem

A sample of what the team put on the whiteboard, and how they grouped it is shown here:

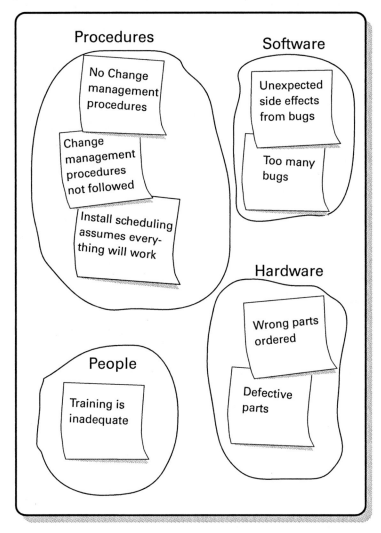

On-time Software Installation Problem: Grouped Sticky Notes

The frame of the Ishikawa looked like this:

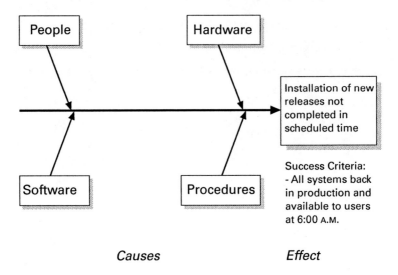

Causes   *Effect*

On-time Software Installation Problem: Ishikawa Frame

Transfer Causes from Sticky Notes to Diagram and Identify Remaining Causes

Copy the causes from the sticky notes into their categories on the diagram. Write each general cause on a line with an arrow pointing to the appropriate category line. Then add more detailed causes that explain why the general cause occurs. These go on lines pointing to that general cause.

Continue to build the structure using brainstorming to identify more

> HINT: *To build the structure, keep asking:*
>
> "Why is this happening?"
>
> "Why aren't we achieving our success criteria now?"

possible causes. As each is mentioned, identify the most logical place for it on the diagram and write it in there. You build the structure and organize the ideas as you go.

The facilitator, or anyone else in the group, may ask questions to clarify what the idea is and to decide where on the diagram to put it. Otherwise, don't discuss the ideas. The normal rules of brainstorming apply: there are no stupid ideas, the facilitator doesn't censor or control the discussion, everyone gets a chance to contribute.

For each cause, ask "why is this happening?" When you get an answer, ask the same question about that answer. To be sure you go deep enough to get to root causes, use the handy rule of thumb and ask "why" five times, thus going five levels deep.

The diagram is complete when either nobody can think of anything else to add or the answers you get are no longer meaningful. In other words, you're done with this step if you're getting silence or ideas that are

- Global (such as the laws of physics),
- Repetitious (already on the diagram), or
- Silly (people are giggling).

Case 1: On-time Shipping Problem

Here's a partially completed Ishikawa diagram as it looks after the sticky note causes have been transferred to the diagram and a few more causes added. As you can see, your team has already changed some of the category names to be a little more general than what you started with. You've also reworded some of the possible causes, with agreement from the team, to clarify what is meant and make them concise enough to fit on the diagram.

Some of the things on the diagram are not causes and there are duplicates. By the time the session is finished, there will be a lot more causes on it and you'll clean up the things that don't belong.

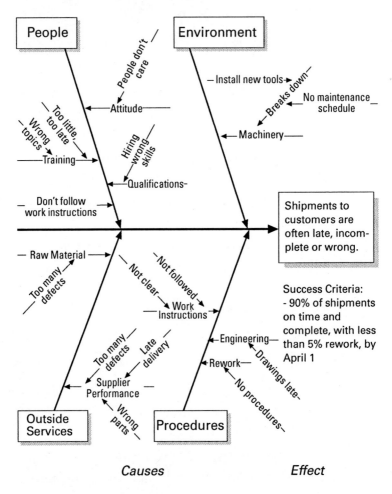

Causes   Effect

On-time Shipping Problem: Partial Ishikawa Diagram

Case 2: On-time Software Installation Problem

Here's a partially completed Ishikawa diagram as it looks after you transferred the sticky note causes to the diagram and the team added a few more causes.

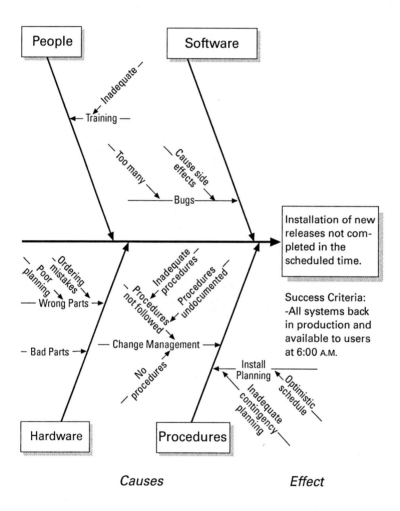

On-time Software Installation Problem: Partial Ishikawa Diagram

Clean Up Diagram

Once the brainstorming is done, the group can review and correct the diagram. You'll want to eliminate anything that is:

- A solution or a task. Only possible causes belong on the diagram, but tasks and solutions tend to creep in. Now is the time to get rid of them. If it's something you know you need to do, put it on your task list. Don't jump ahead—

> HINT: A verb in the phrase usually means the item is a task or solution. These don't belong on an Ishikawa diagram. Take them off.

  you don't know yet how you're going to solve it.
- Not a possible cause of *this* problem. In the heat of a good brainstorm session, it's easy to start coming up with causes of all kinds of problems. They may even be related to your problem, but if eliminating them won't help you achieve your success criteria, they don't belong on this Ishikawa diagram.
- A duplicate. If it's really the same cause, you only need it once. If the wording is ambiguous, clarify it.

This type of cleaning up must be done with the entire group so that if something is taken off the diagram, everyone knows why (and agrees). Before you end the meeting, be sure you understand what everything is that's on the diagram: sometimes the abbreviations and short notations get too cryptic.

Immediately after the session, while you still remember the details, transcribe the diagram to a computer if that wasn't done during the session. Consolidate sparse categories, split dense ones and generally rearrange the diagram physically to make it easier to read. Tell the group you will be doing that, and that you will distribute the cleaned up diagram to them for review.

Case 1: On-time Shipping Problem

When you start cleaning up, you find "work instructions not followed" listed under both the "People" and the "Procedures" categories. The team discusses it, and decides these are really same thing. The team feels both places are logical, but decides to put it under "Procedures."

In contrast, the team decides that material defects have two different aspects and therefore belong on the diagram twice, once as a supplier performance factor (i.e., the parts did not meet specifications), but also there is the possibility that the specifications themselves are not adequate.

Further examination of the diagram shows "install new tools" listed under machinery. You realize this is a possible solution, not a cause, so you asked why might you need new tools.

The answer was "current tools give false readings," so you change the diagram to show that as a possible cause. New tools may turn out to be the right solution, but at this point you're still trying to figure out why the problem is happening. (This is only a partial diagram—

your real one would have many more causes, and would go deeper on each).

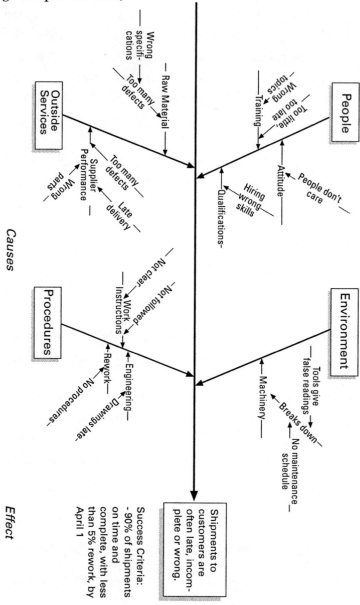

On-time Shipping Problem: Cleaned-up Ishikawa Diagram

Case 2: On-time Software Installation Problem

Process problems such as the ones on this diagram are frequent causes of the kinds of problems that warrant using *SPP*. Inadequate or nonexistent procedures make a regular appearance, but need to be probed by asking "why" until you dig deep enough. Realizing this, you ask the team why the existing procedures are not followed: is it inadequate training (if yes, you want to say so, either in the training part of the diagram or in the procedures part), that the procedures are ignored because they don't work, both, or somthing else? The team decides it is both. You also realize that the change management procedures are inadequate or nonexistent, but can't be both. The team isn't sure which it is, so you leave both on the diagram until you can verify which is really true.

Here's the partially completed Ishikawa diagram as it looks after you clean it up.

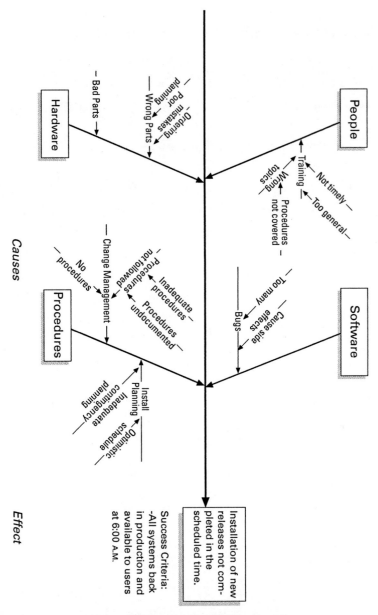

On-time Software Installation Problem:
Cleaned-up Ishikawa Diagram

Do It For Real

You're ready to conduct your Ishikawa session. You will introduce the session, then turn it over to the facilitator, if it's someone other than you, to lead the group through the remaining steps.

1. Introduce the session. If everyone doesn't know each other, do introductions. Review the purpose of the meeting and agenda. Remind everyone what problem you're addressing and what the success criteria are.

2. Identify possible causes. Pass out the sticky notes and have everyone write down their ideas.

3. Group causes and **draw** the diagram frame. Have everyone put their notes on the wall, moving them without talking, into groupings they find natural. Name the groups, then draw the diagram frame.

4. Transfer the causes from the sticky notes to the diagram. Then complete the diagram by having the group **brainstorm** additional causes. Use the "five whys" to be sure you get deep enough.

5. Clean Up the diagram. Make sure everything on the diagram belongs there. Eliminate solutions, actions, duplicates and anything that does not explain *this* problem.

6. Close the session. Thank everyone for their participation and explain what happens next (read ahead so you'll know what to tell them). Remind them why this was worth their time and attention.

7. Finish cleaning up and circulate the diagram to everyone who attended the session for review and correction.

In one meeting, you've completed the largest piece of the analysis step.

Verify the Causes and Set Priorities

The diagram at this point is a collection of possible causes, so the next step is to find out which ones are real. Collect data, devise tests, create process flow charts, or do whatever is necessary to change those possible causes into confirmed causes or eliminate them. The questions to answer are:

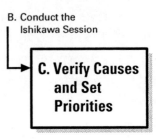

B. Conduct the Ishikawa Session

C. Verify Causes and Set Priorities

Ishikawa Analysis Process Segment

- Is the cause true? For example, a cause on the diagram might be "the technicians weren't trained." It should be easy to verify whether they were. It's not as easy to distinguish if that training, even if poor, was a cause. However, if you don't find out what's really happening, you could invest a lot of effort in changing something only to find your problem is still there.

  There is nothing so deceptive as an apparent truth.

  — Russell Ackoff

- Does the cause on the diagram result in *this* problem? This can also be hard to verify, but if you can prove the connection between the cause and the effect, then you know definitely that eliminating the cause will help achieve your success criteria. It's a much safer position for you and your team than guessing.

Get as close as you can to verifying the causes with facts. Even if you can't positively prove a cause is real, you can and should collect as much evidence as possible. Then you can choose whether or not to address a cause using judgement based on evidence rather than opinion and hearsay.

You may uncover additional causes or redefine causes already on your Ishikawa diagram as a result of your research. If that happens, update your Ishikawa diagram to reflect what you learned.

Most Ishikawa diagrams identify many more causes than are practical to address, at least all at once. However, since your problem is a mess, no single cause will explain why all the interrelated problems occur. Therefore, in addition to validating the causes to make sure they are real, you'll need to set priorities so that you fix the right ones. There are two factors to consider:

- Will eliminating the cause have a big impact on your ability to achieve your success criteria? If yes, make it a high priority for immediate action.
- Will it be easy to eliminate the cause? If yes, make it a high priority, even if the impact will only be moderate. Addressing these "quick-wins" gives you immediate results. This encourages everyone

> HINT: It's not necessary to fix every cause, even if it's real.

involved and gains credibility and support for you and your team. If you have difficulty deciding, try using the assessment matrix described in the next chapter.

Quick-wins often correct symptoms rather than root causes, but still may be worth fixing. Make sure, though, that the impact on your success criteria is big enough to warrant even a relatively small effort to fix.

If removing a cause will have a significant effect on your success criteria or if it's a worthwhile quick-win, fix it. Otherwise, even though the cause may be real, don't waste your time on it. Invest your effort where it will make a difference.

Case 1: On-time Shipping Problem

The team reviews the cleaned up diagram, and decides to work the causes by group. First, the team chooses to treat "Training and Hiring Right People" as one cause because they believe training requirements are dependent on who they are hiring, and vice versa. Since the front line supervisors are on the team, and completely familiar with what happens every day on the floor, the team feels their confirmation is sufficient validation that training and hiring are high priority root causes of this problem.

With a short discussion, the team decides to defer addressing supplier issues because, although the cause is real, defective material is not frequent enough to consider this a high impact cause. (A team member had the data with him, so the team could confirm this on the spot).

After looking at data that shows the majority of late shipments involve rework of some kind, the team decides the lack of rework procedures is a significant cause of delays and expects it to be relatively easy to address. Although eliminating the causes of rework is a key objective, the team feels they don't have enough data yet to confirm what those causes are. Therefore, they agree to build data collection and feedback loops into the new rework procedures so they can start eliminating the causes of rework next.

Case 2: On-time Software Installation Problem

At the end of the Ishikawa session, the team assigns some actions to verify whether there are existing installation planning or change management procedures, and if so, to collect any documentation that exists about what the procedures are. They discover there are installation planning procedures, but they haven't been updated in years and are missing major components such as contingency planning. Real change management procedures are totally absent.

It doesn't take much discussion for the team to agree that these two causes are the most important, and further, that addressing them would probably flush out a number of related issues. This, in turn, will help set priorities for what else should be done.

Do It For Real

Your cleaned up Ishikawa diagram gives you a comprehensive list of possible causes. Use the following steps to figure out which ones are real and which ones you will address first:

1. Decide what level in the diagram you want to work at for each cause. Sometimes it's more convenient to work with a group of related causes. For example, you may have causes that are mutually exclusive such as "inadequate training" and "no training." You can treat them together to verify which it is.

2. Determine how you will verify each cause or group of causes. This becomes your verification plan. Add the tasks of your verification plan to your task list, including owners, due dates and completion criteria.

3. Follow the plan, completing the tasks you identified to verify the causes.

4. Revise the diagram. Eliminate any causes that you determined were either not true or not causes of your current problem. Keep a record of what you eliminated and why so you won't have to retrace these steps if someone brings the cause up again later.

5. Set priorities. For the causes that you confirm are valid, decide which ones you will address first. Mark these on the diagram, using any method that's convenient and clear, such as circling them, changing the type face, or numbering them.

At this point, you've developed substantial documentation that demonstrates what you know about your problem and your problem solving project. You have a completed and agreed-to Problem Statement that defines your problem, an Ishikawa diagram that shows the root causes of your problem, a success criteria report that shows your starting measurements, and an ongoing task list that shows completed and upcoming actions.

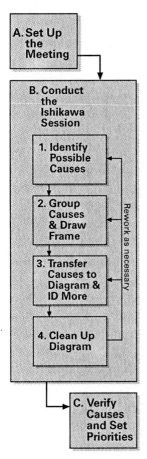

Ishikawa Analysis Process Flow

You've now finished the root cause analysis step of *Solving Problems Permanently*[SM]. You're no longer guessing at what is causing your problem—you *know*. You've verified that the causes are real, and you've decided which ones to fix first. You also have support from the people who are most knowledgeable about the problem because they participated so extensively in determining the causes. You're ready to solve it.

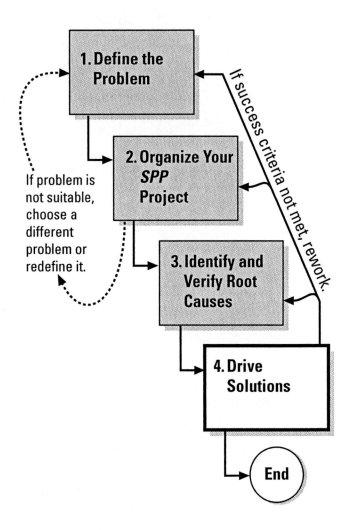

Solving Problems Permanently[SM] Process Flow

Drive Solutions

T his is where everything gets tied together and you start to get results. Because you've verified the causes, you know why your problem occurs. Because you've assessed their impact, you can now focus on and eliminate the important causes, or at least minimize the chances of them occurring. The time you've invested in preparing will now pay off with effective solutions that really will solve the problem.

Develop and Execute Action Plans

You've already started keeping a task list for everything you and your team are doing to make the problem solving project happen. The task list also includes your contingency plans to make sure the vulnerabilities and dependencies don't prevent you from achieving your success criteria.

Now you're going to add the tasks that will actually solve the problem. You'll create an action plan for each cause that you've identified as important enough to address. Add the tasks that make up each cause's action plan to your task list so you can manage them.

Choose the Best Approach

Take the causes one at a time. For each, decide how you will eliminate that cause. In many cases, you will be able to decide with a short discussion. If the best choice is not obvious, start by brainstorming alternative approaches. Then build an assessment matrix to help you decide.

Using an Assessment Matrix

Draw a table, as shown below, with a row for each possible approach in the left column. Make two columns for ratings as shown, and a final column for the score.

Options	Impact	Achievability	Score
Approach A			
Approach B			

Assessment Matrix Template

Assess how likely each approach is to eliminate the cause by rating its impact on a one to five scale, where one is low and five is high. Now assess how achievable the approach is, considering how difficult, expensive and time-consuming it will be to carry out the strategy. One is difficult, five is easy.

The team can determine ratings either by consensus or by averaging individual ratings. To use consensus, discuss the approaches one at a time, first addressing impact and then achievability. Keep talking until the team agrees on the rating. If opinion stays divided or if the list is long, it may be quicker for individuals to fill out the matrix with their own assessment. A team rating is determined by averaging the individual ratings.

You may have trouble deciding because you don't have enough information. In that case, take the time to investigate further and find out what the impact will be or what resources you'll need. If you guess wrong, you won't achieve the expected results and could fail at solving your problem entirely.

If you rated any of the approaches one in impact, eliminate it from further consideration right now. It's not worth bothering with.

> HINT: The assessment matrix is a tool to help you clarify your thinking. It does not make decisions for you.

Once you have agreed-to ratings, you can calculate the scores by multiplying the impact rating times the achievability rating. Perform the multiplication and fill in the scores column. The scores reflect the combined effect of impact and achievability.

If the approaches are mutually exclusive, choose the approach with the highest score. If you are evaluating complementary approaches, you'll want to take the highest scoring approaches first. You will probably also want to choose a threshold and eliminate everything with a score below that threshold from further consideration.

Options	Impact	Achievability	Score
Approach A	4	4	16
Approach B	3	5	15
Approach C	5	2	10

Example Assessment Matrix

In this example, the team would probably choose to implement both approaches A and B if they are complementary, or only approach A if they are mutually exclusive.

Sometimes when you see the scores and the ranking of the approaches, you'll decide you don't agree. In this example, the team might decide they really want to take approach C since it has the highest impact rating. That's ok—the assessment matrix is only a tool to help you decide. It does not make decisions for you. However, in a situation like this, you should think very carefully about achievability and make sure that you can be successful even though it may be hard.

Make It Happen

Now that you know what basic approach you'll take, list the actions that will implement that strategy. Each action is a task, so as before, it must have an owner, due date and completion criteria.

However, the tasks in an action plan are interdependent: together they define how you will eliminate a cause of your problem.

> HINT: Everything necessary, nothing extraneous. Make sure your action plan includes everything you must do to meet your success criteria. Eliminate anything that doesn't contribute to solving *this* problem.

The tasks in an action plan are the necessary steps along the way, but probably won't have much impact in isolation. Cross-check to assure that:

- When the action plan for a particular cause is completed, the cause will be eliminated,
- When all your action plans are completed, you will achieve the success criteria for the whole problem, as defined in your problem statement, and
- Your contingency plans are sufficient to deal with any surprises.

Executing the action plan is simple in concept though not necessarily easy to do. Action plans are dynamic, so you will need to make changes as you proceed. For example, although you'll do everything possible to stay on schedule, eventually something will be late and you won't be able to prevent it. As soon as you find that out, revise the due date so it reflects reality, not wishful thinking. Review all the other actions that follow to see if further revisions are necessary.

Be sure someone, probably you, has the job of managing the action plans as a whole or things will tend to drift apart. The job means you must:

> HINT: Don't let the action plan join the list of good intentions. Now you're at the stage where it's easy to get distracted by other projects. Your problem is important and the risks are still there until you execute an effective action plan.

> HINT: Don't trust luck (or assume everything will go according to plan). If you own the plan, you're responsible for the results —make sure it happens.

- Check on everything and everyone (tactfully),

- Offer help, remove roadblocks or escalate if necessary, and
- Adjust the plans as you go, watching out for dependencies.

Case 1: On-time Shipping Problem

The team had decided to address two key cause groups: "Training and Hiring Right People" and "Rework Procedures." In both cases, the first steps in the action plans are to gather more information because you don't know enough yet to really start corrective action.

For the Training/Hiring group, although the team is convinced that training/hiring is a real issue, the detailed, specific causes still need to be verified. Therefore the initial tasks are to determine what skills are required for the job. This is a necessary first step to address either training or hiring concerns.

For the Rework Procedures, the first task is to gather detailed information about what aspects of handling rework are in the worst shape. Here is the revised Task List showing the initial action plans to start addressing each of these tasks.

Task	Completion Criteria	Owner	Due Date
Project Management Develop project schedule	1st version accepted by team	Ops. Dir.	complete
Hold progress review team meeting	Meeting held	Ops. Dir.	11/21

(List continues)

Task	Completion Criteria	Owner	Due Date
Measurement Plan			
Design success criteria reports	Reports approved by team and by Pres.	Production Supervisor	complete
Set up measurement procedures	Report completed using new procedures	Production Supervisor	complete
Communication Plan			
Identify proposed recipients for success critiera report, invite participation, and create distribution list	First report distributed	Ops. Dir.	11/21
Action Plan: Training & Hiring Right People			
Create job criteria (skills required for each level for each type of job)	Management signs off	Production Supervisor	11/21
Assess current skill level & training requirements for each employee	Supervisors sign off	Each Super.	11/21
Action Plan: Rework Procedures			
Collect rework data by work area	Pareto chart enables team to choose focus areas	Production Supervisor	11/21

On-time Shipping Problem: Task List with Initial Action Plans

Case 2: On-time Software Installation Problem

You had decided to start by addressing two key cause groups: "Install Planning Procedures" and "Change Management Procedures." Although there are some existing procedures for installations, they are so badly out-of-date that the team readily decides it is safer and easier to start over. This is an easy decision, so you don't need to use an assessment matrix to decide whether to modify the existing procedures or start fresh.

With these decisions made, the tasks necessary to create and implement the new procedures are quite straightforward to identify. The following part of the task list shows how the team starts to address these two root causes.

Task	Completion Criteria	Owner	Due Date
Action Plan: Create Change Management Process			
Establish process definition, triggers, metrics	Documentation accepted by team	Ops. Mgr. Site B	4/7
Create criteria for acceptable changes, scheduling requirements, etc.	Criteria accepted by site Ops. Mgrs. & DAS	Ops. Mgr. Site A	4/5
Action Plan: Create Installation Planning Procedures			
Define metrics for a successful installation	Metrics accepted by Site Mgrs. & Ops. Director	Yu	4/7

On-time Software Installation Problem:
Task List with Initial Action Plans

Do It For Real

Build and execute the action plan to solve your problem:

1. Choose an approach, or strategy, for eliminating each cause. If necessary, use the assessment matrix to choose.

2. Decide the tasks to implement each strategy. This is your action plan for each cause. If you don't know enough to decide the whole action plan, write down as many of the details as you can and outline the rest. Fill in more as you learn more.

3. Recheck your contingency plans for managing vulnerabilities and dependencies. Now that you know how you're going to solve the problem, go back and review these. Make sure they are complete and reasonable.

4. Cross-check everything. Make sure your action plans include *everything necessary, nothing extraneous.* If necessary, back up to previous steps and rethink what you're doing.

5. Execute the action plans, adjusting and filling in details as you go. Remember to execute your communication plan so everyone knows what's happening and won't waste your time with individual requests for progress reports. Your work must be visible to be recognized.

Measure Results

Measuring your success criteria is an ongoing activity throughout your problem solving project, but it also tells you when you are finished. When you achieve your success criteria, your problem is solved and the project is done. The team can disband and go on to other projects. Until then, the problem remains unsolved and, unless priorities have changed and it has become unimportant, the team must keep working on choosing and eliminating root causes.

Once you start executing your action plan, every time you review your measurements until you achieve your success criteria, you will ask:

- Do the measurements show improvement, that is, are we getting closer to achieving our success criteria?
- If yes, are we as close as we think we should be, given the actions that have been taken so far?

If either answer is no, you must investigate to figure out why. Start working backwards, checking everything. Is something missing in an action plan? Should you reconsider the approach? If the action plans are sound, check the root cause analysis step.

Are you addressing the right causes? Is an important key root cause missing from the Ishikawa diagram? What about the problem definition itself? Are you working on the right problem, and do your success criteria measure it properly? Has some influential factor changed since you started?

If you're stuck, try applying the *SPP* process to the new problem of why the solutions you identified aren't working. As with any other problem, taking this systematic approach can help you understand what is behind your lack of results.

When your problem is solved, it's time to clean up any odds and ends such as completing any remaining action items, assessing the effort and making sure the project documentation is complete and filed appropriately. Then publicize the results, have a celebration and move on to your next projects.

A key part of concluding a project and improving your skills as a problem solver is to analyze how the effort itself went. Perform a plus/minus (+ / −) assessment on the project as a whole. Pluses are the things you and the team did right; minuses are the things you will do differently next time.

> HINT: Ask yourself:
> What worked?
> What didn't work? Why?
> What could you do to make solving your next problem quicker, easier and more effective?

Ask the team to participate, write it down, and review it before starting a new project. For example, the following demonstrates part of a plus/minus assessment of an *SPP* project.

+	−
Cooperation among team members	Sponsor not really committed
Success criteria well defined —helped get buy-in and understanding of problem	Schedule too optimistic
	Communication plan took several attempts before it worked

Example Plus/Minus Assessment

Announcing and celebrating your achievement is particularly important. Solving an important problem deserves recognition, and nobody else is going to take care of this for you. Make sure the sponsor and the other key stakeholders know what you and your team have achieved. Remind them of the risks avoided. Tell them how much money you saved the company.

Thank your team members and everyone else who helped make your project successful. Decide what sort of celebration is appropriate, given the importance of the problem and the way your company recognizes significant achievements. Then make sure it happens.

Case 1: On-time Shipping Problem

As the team begins implementing corrective actions, you see improvements in the success criteria metrics immediately, which demonstrates to everyone that you are on the right track. The final reports show, though there were some difficulties along the way, the team solved the problem.

The President was ecstatic when he saw the results, and made a point of personally going to each member of the team and thanking them for their participation. A luncheon was also held for everyone who participated in the project in any way.

Although the team met your success criteria, you, as Operations Director, will continue to check these measurements on an ongoing basis. This is necessary to prove that the problem is truly solved and that the good measurements weren't one-time luck. It is also necessary to keep monitoring so that, if the rates slip in the future, you will know about it immediately. If this happens, CRF will be able to find out why and correct the problem— before things are so bad that customers start complaining again.

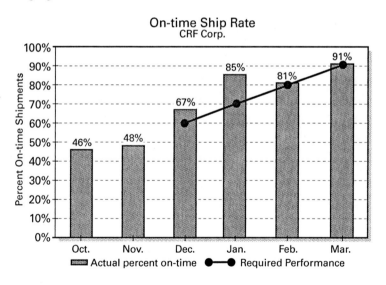

On-time Shipping Problem: Final Success Criteria Report

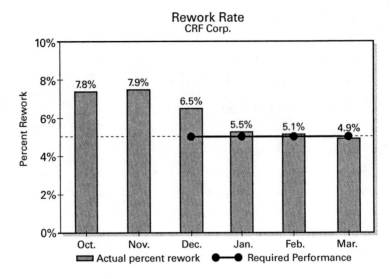

On-time Shipping Problem: Final Success Criteria Report

Case 2: On-time Software Installation Problem

The team got a chance to test your corrective actions installing a software release at the end of May. Although there were more hardware changes you wanted to make as well, the new procedures limited each installation to a single change. This would eliminate the risk that changes would interfere with each other and cause a failure to meet success criteria. It also would make it much easier to analyze what went wrong if there were problems.

Of course, one successful installation does not prove the problem is solved permanently, but it's an excellent indication of real progress on an urgent problem. The team agrees that they will continue to work on action plans and monitor the results until September and, assuming the results continue on the desired path, plan a celebration then.

Installation Report Card			
Description	**Date**	**Pass/Fail**	**Comments**
Install v. 3.1.7 DAS software (bug fixes & new features). Install new disk drives	3/23	F	Full production 6 hours late. Software not ready until noon; disk drive ready at 8:00 A.M. Action: YU heading *SPP* project to find out why and fix.
Install v. 3.1.8 DAS software (bug fixes)	5/29	P	Full production at 5:55 A.M. Success criteria met, but too close. Action: *SPP* project to complete implementing corrective actions.

On-time Software Installation Problem: Success Criteria Report

Do It For Real

Prove that your problem is solved to everyone who cares:

1. Measure your success criteria. If you're not done, keep working. If you've solved the problem, go on to the next step.

2. Announce the results. This is a good time to thank everyone publicly who contributed to the effort.

3. Clean up. Finish any actions still incomplete that will improve your results enough to be worth doing. Make sure the written records are complete, and file them so you or another team can retrieve them if necessary.

4. Analyze your project using plus/minus assessment. Identify what worked well and what you will do differently next time.

5. Celebrate a job well done.

6. Start your next project.

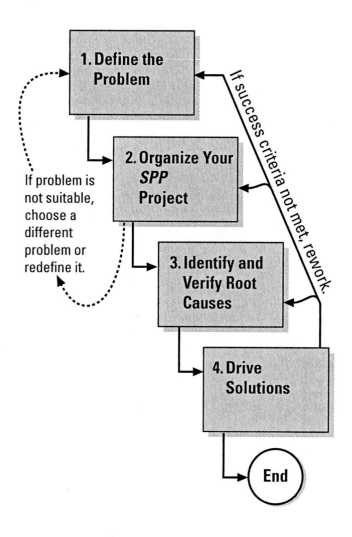

Solving Problems Permanently[SM] Process Flow

Appendix

The Appendix includes tools to make your problem solving easier. Here you will find templates for the problem worksheet and for your task list. You may photocopy these or make a version on your computer to use in your problem solving projects.

Use the *SPP* Checklist to cross-check that you've really completed each step in the *SPP* process. The *SPP* Steps Summary is a reminder of what to do as you proceed through your problem solving process. You can use these steps as the outline of the tasks in your project plan.

Problem Worksheet

Use the following as a template for your problem statement. Fill in each section, using the space you need. However, keep it concise: the whole thing shouldn't be more than two pages, and usually one is enough.

Solving Problems Permanently^{SM}
Problem Worksheet

Problem Description

Sponsor

Analyst

Success Criteria

Key Characteristics

   Who (key players)

   Where

   When

Risks and Vulnerabilities

   Risks

   Vulnerabilities

   Dependencies

Task List Template

Use the following template for your task list. Include whatever sections make sense for your problem, but you'll always have a section for tasks to:

1. Manage your problem solving project,

2. Create and execute your measurement plan,

3. Create and execute your contingency plans, and

4. Implement action plans to eliminate each of the root causes you've selected.

Task	Completion Criteria	Owner	Due Date
Project Management			
Measurement Plan			
Communication Plan			
Contingency Plans: [one plan for each vulnerability you are addressing]			
Action Plans: [one plan for each root cause you are addressing]			

SPP Checklist

Use this checklist to cross-check each part of a problem solving project. The answers to the questions in each section should be "yes" before you go on to the next phase of the analysis.

1. Define the Problem

Write the Problem Statement

Problem Description
- ☐ Does it describe the correct problem?
- ☐ Is it clear and unambiguous? Can someone who doesn't already know understand correctly what you'll be addressing—and not addressing?
- ☐ Is it concise?
- ☐ Is the problem manageable?

Sponsor and Analyst
- ☐ Have you identified the problem sponsor?
- ☐ Does the sponsor have a vested interest in solving the problem? Is the sponsor generally respected? Are you confident that he or she will be a strong champion for you?
- ☐ Can and will the sponsor allocate resources and remove roadblocks?
- ☐ Have you identified an analyst with the necessary skills?
- ☐ Is the analyst considered competent and unbiased by the sponsor and other key players?

Success Criteria

☐ When the success criteria are met, will you, your colleagues and your customer truly consider the problem solved?

☐ Do the success criteria ask for more than is necessary to solve *this* problem?

☐ Is each criterion SMARTI? Check "I" for Importance first: if it's not important, take it out entirely.

☐ Do the success criteria match the problem description?

Key Characteristics

☐ Have you identified everyone who will participate in your problem solving project? Do you know what their roles and responsibilities will be?

☐ Have you identified stakeholders who must commit resources to the project?

☐ Have you identified and listed any other characteristics that will define your project?

Risks, Vulnerabilities and Dependencies

☐ Are the risks and vulnerabilities adequately identified?

☐ Are the dependencies clear?

Complete the Problem Statement

☐ Have you cross-checked everything for completeness and consistency?

- ☐ Can you actually collect and report the measurements you've defined? Do they tell you what you need to know?
- ☐ Have you established your baseline measurements?

2. Organize Your *SPP* Project

Get Commitment and Sponsorship

- ☐ Is the problem important enough to solve? What's the business impact of the problem vs the expected cost of resolution?
- ☐ Is it complicated enough to need *SPP*? Is it well defined and small enough to be manageable?
- ☐ Do you have commitment from the sponsor and other stakeholders to proceed?
- ☐ Do you have agreement from the other participants to fulfill their roles?

Set Up Your Project Plan

- ☐ Does your task list have everything on it that you can think of so far?
- ☐ Is your communication plan in place? Do you know what information you will be distributing, to whom, when and how?
- ☐ Have you developed contingency plans to address vulnerabilities and dependencies?
- ☐ Have you set up a realistic project schedule?
- ☐ Do you have the resources you need to proceed?

Establish Your Measurement Plan

- ☐ Do you know what you will measure?
- ☐ Have you designed your reports?
- ☐ Do you know how you will collect the data and produce the reports?

3. Identify and Verify Root Causes

Set Up the Meeting

- ☐ Are all the right people identified and have they agreed to participate in the Ishikawa session? Have you chosen a facilitator and has that person accepted the role?
- ☐ Is the analysis session scheduled? Have you allowed enough time?
- ☐ Are appropriate facilities reserved for the meeting?

Conduct the Ishkawa Session

- ☐ Did you complete an Ishikawa diagram? Are you confident that it includes all the possible causes?
- ☐ Is the documentation complete and distributed to everyone appropriate?

Verify Causes and Set Priorities

- ☐ Have you determined which causes are real causes of *this* problem and eliminated any that aren't?

☐ Have you decided which causes you will address first?

4. Drive Solutions

Develop and Execute Action Plans

☐ Are action plans in place to address each cause you've chosen to address—with ownership, due dates and completion criteria?

☐ Are the owners capable (right position, right skills, enough time/resources) of getting their actions completed successfully and on time?

☐ Will the actions you've identified achieve the success criteria on your problem statement?

☐ Do you have adequate contingency plans to address the vulnerabilities on your problem statement, and are you executing them?

☐ Do you have adequate plans to manage the dependencies?

Measure Results

☐ Are you following your measurement plan?

☐ Do the data show progress?

☐ Have you met your success criteria?

Celebrate success

☐ Have you publicly acknowledged everyone who helped?

☐ Have you announced the results so that "everyone" knows about your team's success?

☐ Was the party fun?

SPP Steps Summary

Use this summary of the *SPP* steps as a reminder of what to do as you proceed through your project.

> HINT: You can use this summary of the SPP steps to start your task list.

Define the Problem

Write the Problem Description

1. Brainstorm possible topic sentences.
2. Discuss the pros and cons of each.
3. Choose the best and revise.
4. Write the rest of the description.
5. Sanity check.
6. Revise again.

Identify the Sponsor and Analyst

1. Identify your preferred sponsor and analyst.

Establish Success Criteria

1. Build the framework.
2. Refine until everything is covered and it's unambiguous.
3. Cross-check with the problem description.
4. Sanity check, revise and add to your worksheet.

Describe Key Characteristics

1. Identify the key players and their roles.
2. Describe the geographic scope.
3. Describe when the problem occurred.
4. Describe anything else relevant to your problem.

Determine Risks, Vulnerabilities and Dependencies

1. Brainstorm possibilities for each category.
2. Discuss and revise.

Complete the Problem Worksheet

1. Check each section individually.
2. Cross-check sections with each other.
3. Verify with real data to establish baselines and check reasonableness of success criteria.
4. Revise.

Organize Your *SPP* Project

Get Commitment and Sponsorship

1. Verify that you personally believe the problem is worth solving and that you can meet the success criteria.
2. Get commitment from the sponsor and other key players to participate.

Set Up Your Project Plan

1. Start your task list.
2. Establish communication plan.
3. Develop contingency plans.
4. Develop the project schedule.
5. Estimate and get resources allocated.
6. Cross-check everything.
7. Confirm assignments.
8. Update everything as you proceed.

Establish Your Measurement Plan

1. Design your success criteria report.
2. Implement data collection and reporting.
3. Update your communication plan.

Identify and Verify Root Causes

Set Up the Meeting

1. Decide on scheduling and facilities.
2. Invite everyone necessary.
3. Remind them of the time, place and purpose of the session.
4. Check the room to make sure everything is set up correctly.

Conduct the Ishikawa Session

1. Introduce the session.
2. Identify possible causes.
3. Group causes and draw frame.
4. Transfer causes to diagram and brainstorm more.
5. Clean up the diagram.
6. Close the session.
7. Finish cleaning up the diagram for final review.

Verify Causes and Set Priorities

1. Decide how to group causes to work with them most easily.
2. Determine a verification plan and execute it.
3. Revise the diagram.
4. Set priorities.

Drive Solutions

Develop and Execute Action Plans

1. Choose an approach for each cause.
2. Decide actions and add to task list.
3. Recheck plans for vulnerabilities and dependencies.
4. Cross-check to assure action plans include everything necessary, nothing extraneous.
5. Do it: execute the action plans.

Measure Results

1. Measure success criteria, backing up to previous steps as necessary.
2. Announce the results (when you've achieved success) and thank everyone who participated.
3. Clean up.
4. Analyze project using plus/minus.
5. Celebrate.
6. Start something new.

Glossary

Action Plan

A group of coordinated tasks that must be completed to accomplish something, such as eliminate a problem cause.

Analyst

The individual responsible for leading a problem solving project.

Apparent Cause

Immediately obvious cause of the symptom. An apparent cause may also be a root cause, but root causes are usually deeper.

Assessment Matrix

A structured tool for determining priorities among multiple approaches or for choosing among mutually exclusive alternatives.

Brainstorming

An informal method to help groups generate as many ideas as possible in a short period of time.

Cause-and-Effect Diagram	Another commonly used name for Ishikawa diagrams.
Completion Criteria	Success criteria for determining successful completion of an action plan or task.
Deliverable	Tangible result of completing a task, e.g., a report or document, product, filled out form.
Dependencies	Other projects or efforts that either depend on or must be coordinated with your problem solving project, or that your project is dependent on.
Fishbone Diagram	Another commonly used name for Ishikawa diagrams.
Ground Rules	Rules agreed to by a group to govern their behavior during a meeting.
Ishikawa Diagram	The diagram that results from performing the root cause analysis technique developed by Kaoru Ishikawa. Also called cause-and-effect diagram and fishbone diagram.

Key Characteristics   Basic information about the problem and environment that help evaluate appropriateness of the problem for root cause analysis and identify resources required for the problem solving project. Key characteristics include who the key players are, the geographic scope of the problem and a description of the time frame of the problem occurrences.

Mess   A system of interrelated problems. Messes are solved by unraveling the complexities using a systematic method such as *SPP*.

Owner   The person responsible for "getting it done," where "it" may be an action plan or individual task.

Parking Lot   A tool used to keep meetings focused on the agenda. The parking lot is a list of off-agenda topics that come up during a meeting, and should be dealt with at some other time. The parking lot is cleared at the end of the meeting by deciding when and how to deal with each item, such as assigning it to someone or putting it on the agenda for a future meeting.

Pareto Chart   A bar chart where the bars show frequency or impact of some event by categories. The bars are shown in order of frequency, with the highest (most significant) on the left.

Plus/Minus (+ / −)   A method to analyze how a project (or meeting) was conducted. Pluses are things that contributed to the project success; minuses are things that you will change next time.

Problem Description   Prose or bullet explanation of what the problem solving effort is to address.

Problem Statement   The written definition of the problem to be solved. It serves as an agreement between the sponsor and the problem solving team, specifying what will be accomplished and how the results will be measured.

Risks   The negative impact on your business if you don't resolve a problem.

Root Cause
Analysis (RCA)

A systematic process to find out "why," or identify the root causes of a problem.

Root Cause

The most basic cause of an undesirable condition, event, or problem.

SMARTI

Acronym/memory hook for characteristics of good success criteria: Specific, Measurable, Appropriate, Reasonable, Time-bound and Important.

Solving Problems Permanently^{SM} *(SPP)*

A systematic method for solving complicated problems. It includes defining the problem carefully, organizing a project to manage the problem solving effort, analyzing the problem for root causes, executing action plans to eliminate the causes and measuring the results.

Sponsor

The individual, usually an executive or senior manager, who champions a problem solving project by authorizing it, allocating resources, removing roadblocks and generally making it possible for the project to succeed.

Subject Matter Expert	An individual with specific expertise, e.g., about a particular product, who can execute specific tasks or make a particular contribution to the Ishikawa session.
Success Criteria	The measurements that tell you when you are done, i.e., the problem is solved.
Symptom	Tangible evidence or manifestation(s) indicating the existence or occurrence of a problem.
Task List	The "to do" list for the analyst and problem solving team of the tasks that must be completed to successfully complete the problem solving project.
Trigger	An action or event that makes a problem occur.
Trouble-shooting	A "trial-and-error" method for solving problems that is effective for simple problems. Experience typically guides decisions about what to try. The problem is assumed to be solved if the symptoms disappear.

Vulnerabilities   Things that could prevent your problem solving project from succeeding, i.e., possible obstacles to the effort of solving the problem.

Reading List

Andersen, Bjørn and Tom Fagerhaug. *Root Cause Analysis: Simplified Tools and Techniques.* Milwaukee, WI: ASQ Quality Press, 2000.

Arnold, John D. *The Complete Problem Solver: A Total System for Competitive Decision Making.* New York: John Wiley & Sons, 1992.

Brassard, Michael. *The Memory Jogger Plus +*™. Methuen, NJ: GOAL/QPC, 1989.

Ishikawa, Kaoru. "Chapter 3: Cause-and-effect diagram (CE diagram)." In *Guide to Quality Control,* 18–29. New York: Asian Productivity Organization, 1982.

Juran, J. M. *Juran's Quality Control Handbook.* New York: McGraw-Hill, 1988. Section 22.26-74.

Sawyer, Jeanne. "Leveraging a Crisis: How to Learn the Truth About What Really Happened and Use It to Change How You Do Business." *The Professional Journal,* **23,** no. 5 (1998): 43–47.

Sawyer, Jeanne. "Managing Yourself and Your Vendors to Avoid a Crisis." *The Professional Journal,* **21,** no. 9 (1997): 13–15. Also in *High-Technology Services,* **21,** no. 9 (1997): 13–15.

Sawyer, Jeanne. "Partnership by Design." *Business and Economic Review,* 44, no. 1 (October–December 1997): 22–25.

Sawyer, Jeanne. "Solving the Right Problem: Using Metrics Effectively." *High-Technology Services Management,* **3,** no. 2, (February 1997): 36-38. Also in *The Professional Journal,* **18,** no. 7 (February 1994): 36–38.

Sawyer, Jeanne. "'Stuff' Doesn't Just Happen: Using the Truth to Prevent Unwanted Incidents and Speed Recovery." *The Professional Journal,* **19,** no. 2 (September 1994): 92–95.

Schottes, Peter R. *The Team Handbook,* 2nd revised edition. Wisconsin: Oriel, Inc., 1996.

Wilson, Paul F., et al. *Root Cause Analysis: A Tool for Total Quality Management.* Wisconsin: ASCQ Quality Press, 1993.

Index

A

Accuracy
    as success characteristic 43
Achievablity rating 120–122
Russell Ackoff 112
Action plan 73, 75, 119–124, 139, 149
Affinity diagram 97
Analyst
    agreement 40
    commitment 40
    definition 39, 149
    role 39, 74, 90, 92, 149, 154
    selection 39–40
Apparent cause 103, 149
Appendix 137–148
Assessment
    matrix 114, 120–122, 149
    plus/minus 129, 152
    priority 113, 120–122

B

Baseline 59, 80
BigTel. *See* On-time Software Installation Problem
Brainstorm
    definition 37, 149
    Ishikawa session 88, 102–103

C

D

K

M

O

T

V

W

About the Author

Consultant, teacher and writer, Jeanne Sawyer has saved her clients millions of dollars and kept them off the front pages by solving messy, expensive, chronic problems—the kind of problems that cause customers to make angry phone calls to executives or even to take their business elsewhere. Her pragmatic approach to solving problems demonstrates measurable results.

Jeanne developed her techniques by combining what she learned from the formal disciplines of computer science and quality with the experience of solving real problems. She holds a Ph.D. and M.S. in computer science and an M.S. in library science from the University of North Carolina at Chapel Hill. Her bachelor's degree in chemistry is from Duke University.

As a result of her *When Stuff Happens* workshops, people have improved their problem solving skills, reduced frustration in their work environment, saved their companies money, and in some cases, saved their jobs. Workshop participants wanted a reference after the workshop, and a guide for their colleagues who didn't get to go. They urged Jeanne to write a book: you're holding the result in your hands.

If you feel that your team or friend(s) might benefit from using this book, please check with your local bookstore or online bookseller to purchase additional copies.

For information on how to bring Jeanne's *When Stuff Happens* workshops to your company, call 408-929-3622.

Visit our website at www.SawyerPartnership.com for free information such as problem solving tips and quotes. Check out Jeanne's published articles for other useful ideas.

For more than 10 copies, please contact the publisher for quantity rates.

The Sawyer Partnership
1241 Renraw Drive
San Jose, CA 95127-4418
Tel. 408-929-3622
Fax. 408-929-5515
Email: bookinfo@sawyerpartnership.com

or see our Web Site at **www.SawyerPartnership.com**

Printed in the United States
29753LVS00002B/37-39